EASY GUITAR
WITH NOTES & TAB

blink-182
GREATEST HITS

ISBN 978-1-4234-6750-2

Hal•Leonard®
CORPORATION
7777 W. BLUEMOUND RD. P.O. BOX 13819 MILWAUKEE, WI 53213

Visit Hal Leonard Online at
www.halleonard.com

Carousel

Words and Music by Scott Raynor, Mark Hoppus and Tom De Longe

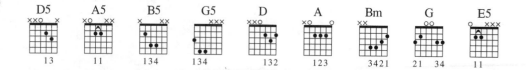

D5   A5   B5   G5   D   A   Bm   G   E5

13   11   134   134   132   123   3421   21 34   11

Strum Pattern: 1, 4
Pick Pattern: 2

Intro
Moderately fast Rock

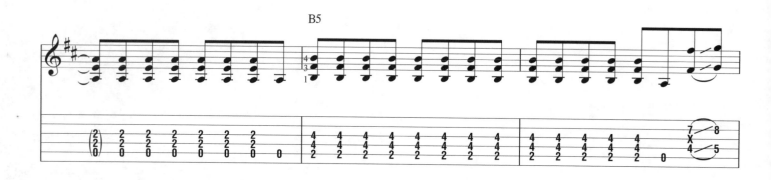

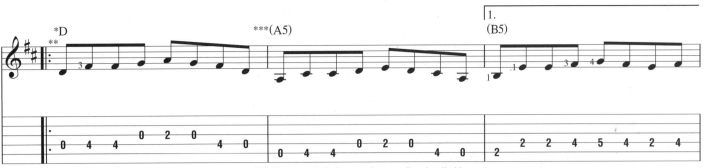

*Let D chord ring, next 8 meas.

***Chord symbols in parentheses reflect implied harmony.

**Bass arr. for gtr., next 16 meas.

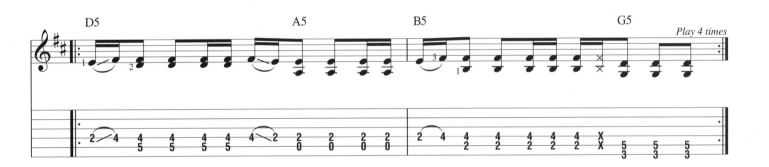

Play 4 times

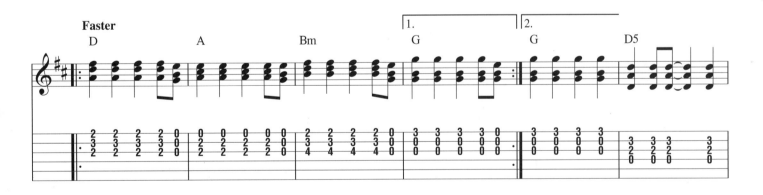

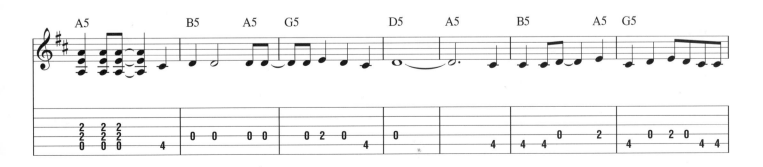

Verse

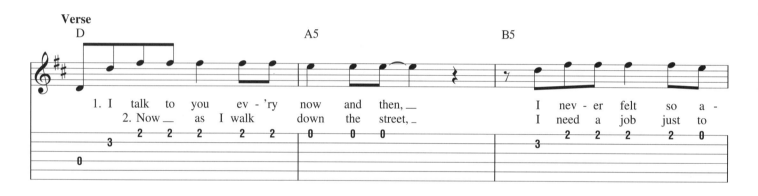

1. I talk to you ev - 'ry now and then, ___ I nev - er felt so a -
2. Now ___ as I walk down the street, ___ I need a job just to

To Coda 1

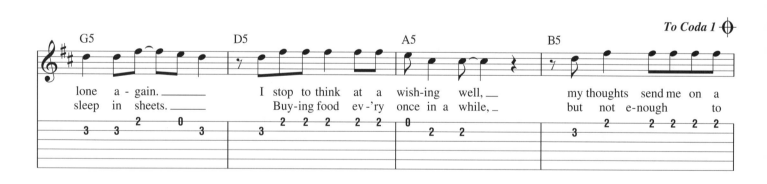

lone a - gain. _____ I stop to think at a wish-ing well, ___ my thoughts send me on a
sleep in sheets. _____ Buy-ing food ev -'ry once in a while, _ but not e-nough to

car - ou - sel. Here I am stand-ing on ___ my own, not a mo-tion from the tel - e -

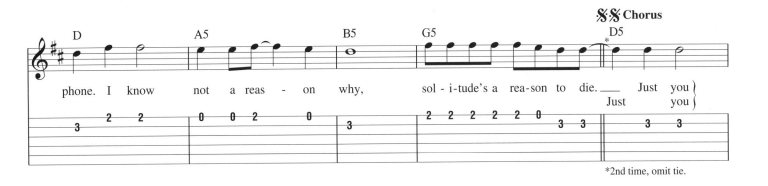

*2nd time, omit tie.

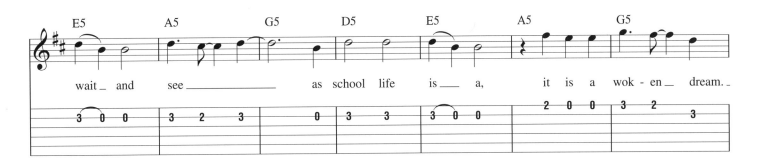

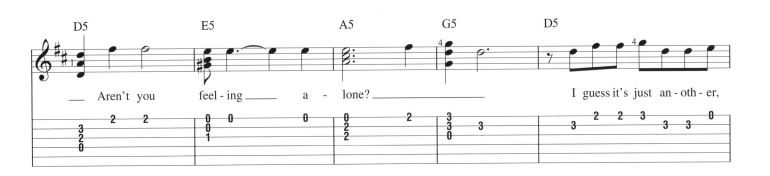

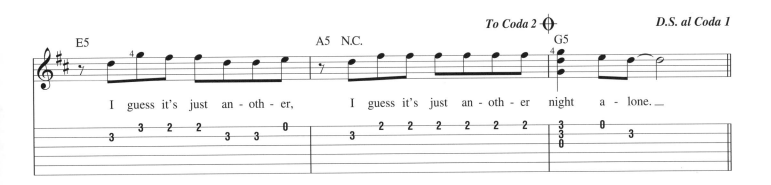

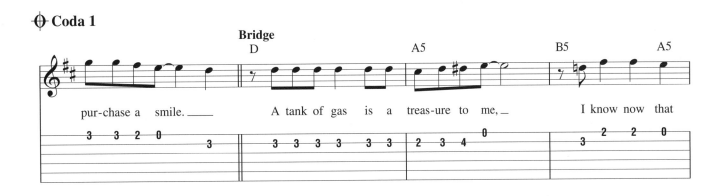

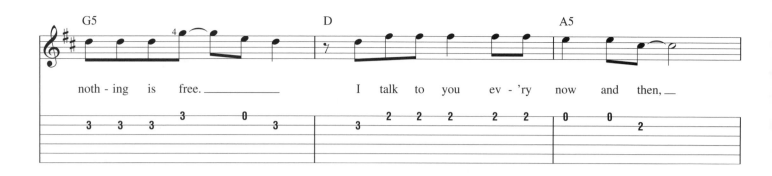

noth - ing is free.＿＿＿＿ I talk to you ev - 'ry now and then, ＿

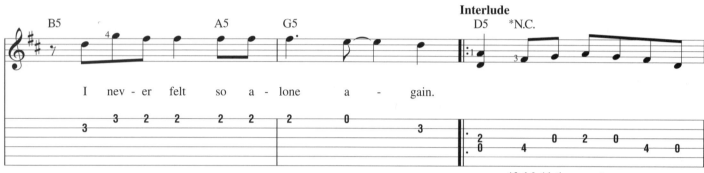

Interlude

I nev - er felt so a - lone a - gain.

*3rd & 4th times, no stops.

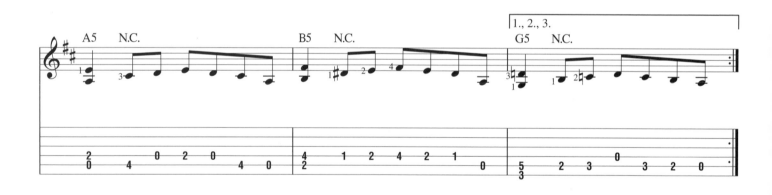

1., 2., 3.

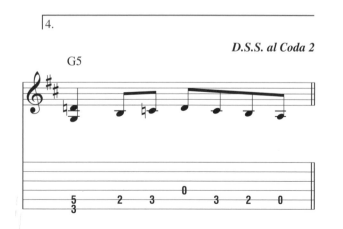

4.

D.S.S. al Coda 2

$\oplus$ **Coda 2**

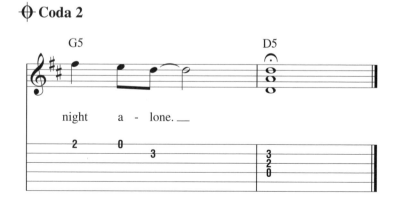

night a - lone. ＿

Josie

Words and Music by Scott Raynor, Mark Hoppus and Tom De Longe

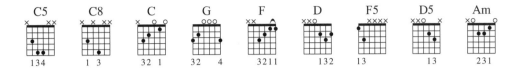

*Tune down 1/2 step:
(low to high) E♭-A♭-D♭-G♭-B♭-E♭

Strum Pattern: 3
Pick Pattern: 3

Intro
Fast Rock

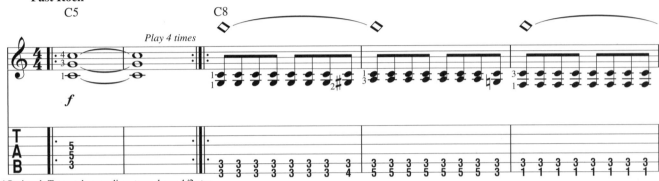

*Optional: To match recording, tune down 1/2 step.

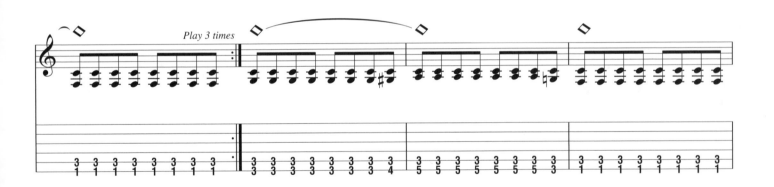

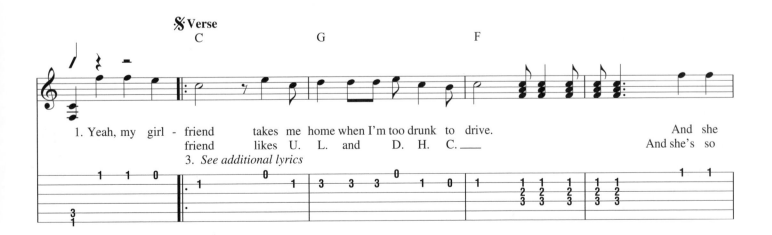

1. Yeah, my girl - friend   takes me home when I'm too drunk to drive.   And she
   friend   likes U. L. and D. H. C. ___   And she's so

3. *See additional lyrics*

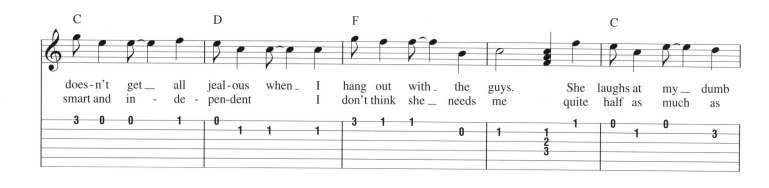

does-n't get __ all jeal-ous when __ I hang out with __ the guys. She laughs at my __ dumb
smart and in - de - pen-dent I don't think she __ needs me quite half as much as

jokes when no __ one does. She brings me Mex - i - can food from Som-brer-o just be-
I know I __ need her. I won - der why there's not __ an - oth - er

cause, yeah, just be - cause. _____ 2. And my girl - guy that she'd __ pre - fer.
cause. And

Pre-Chorus

when I feel like giv - ing up, like __ my world is fall - ing down,

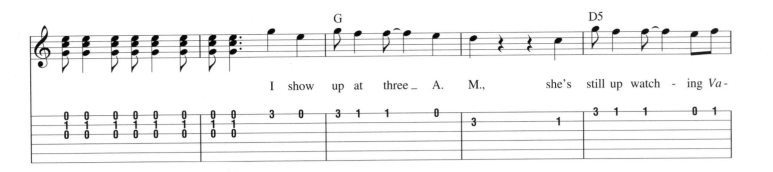

I show up at three __ A. M., she's still up watch - ing Va-

ca - *tion,* and I see her pret - ty face, __ it takes me a - way to a

Chorus

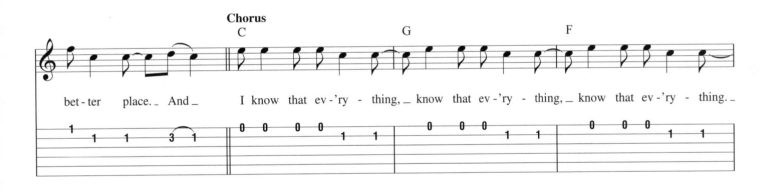

bet - ter place. __ And __ I know that ev -'ry - thing, __ know that ev -'ry - thing, __ know that ev -'ry - thing. __

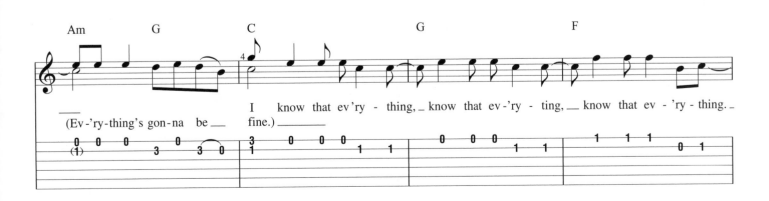

__ (Ev -'ry-thing's gon-na be __ fine.) _____ I know that ev'ry - thing, __ know that ev -'ry - ting, __ know that ev 'ry - thing. __

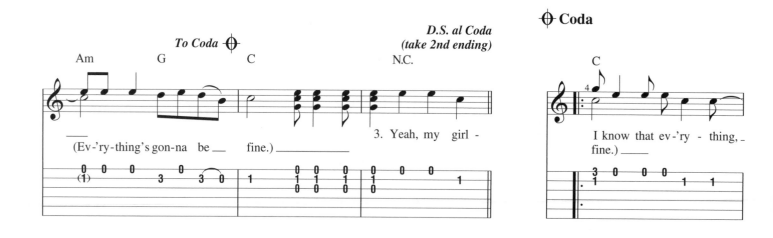

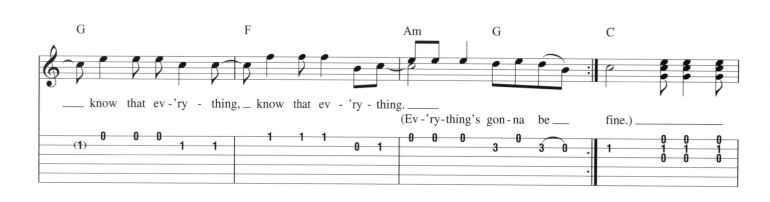

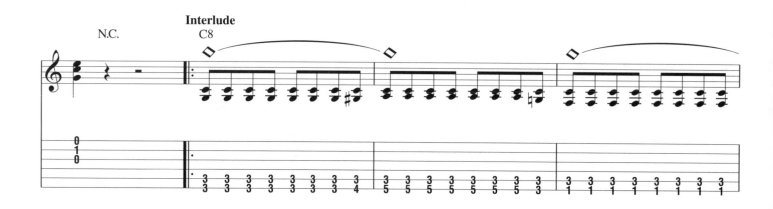

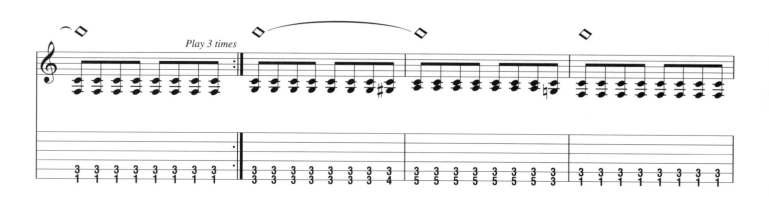

Outro-Chorus

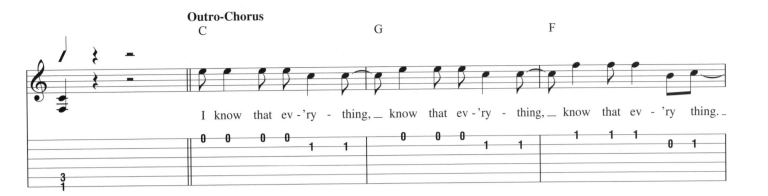

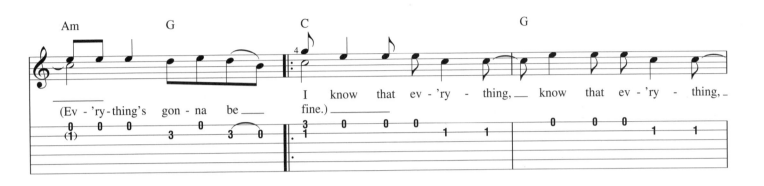

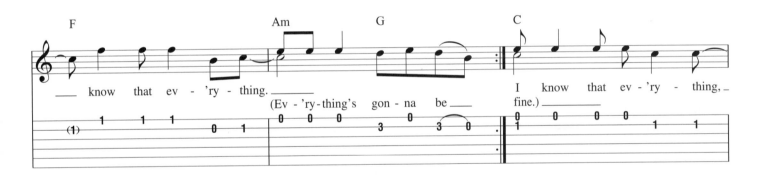

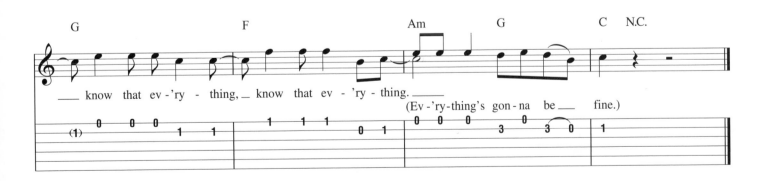

Additional Lyrics

3. Yeah, my girlfriend takes collect calls from the road.
   And it doesn't seem to matter that I'm lacking in the bulge.
   She laughs at my dumb jokes when no one does.
   She brings me Mexican food from Sombrero just because.

M&M

Words and Music by Scott Raynor, Mark Hoppus and Tom De Longe

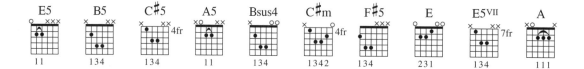

Strum Pattern: 1, 3
Pick Pattern: 4, 5

Intro
Fast Rock

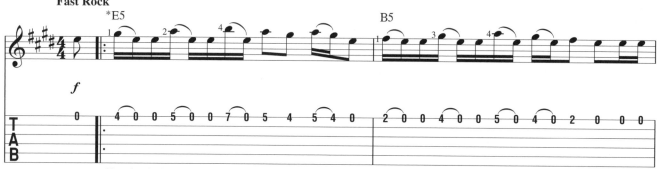

*Let chords ring, next 8 meas.

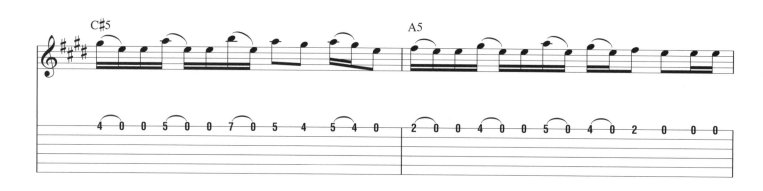

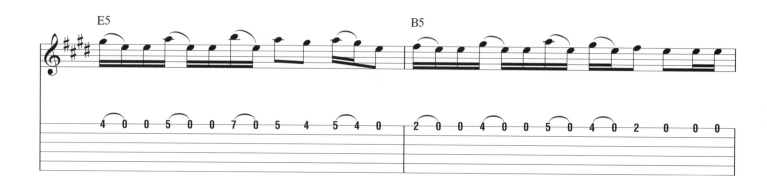

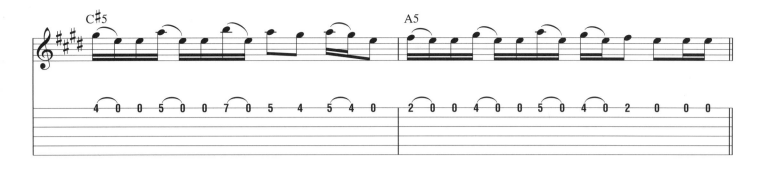

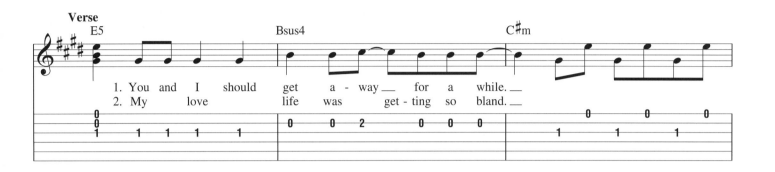

1. You and I should get a - way __ for a while. __
2. My love life was get - ting so bland. __

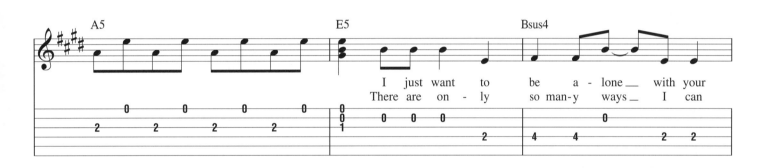

I just want to be a - lone __ with your
There are on - ly so man - y ways __ I can

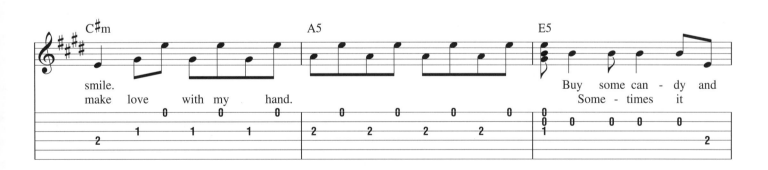

smile. Buy some can - dy and
make love with my hand. Some - times it

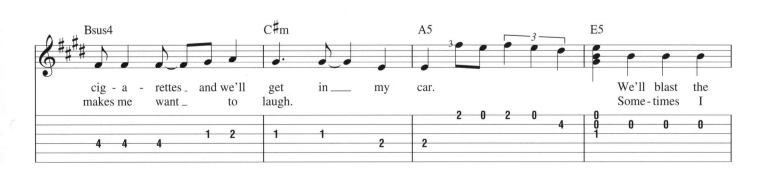

cig - a - rettes __ and we'll get in __ my car. We'll blast the
makes me want __ to laugh. Some - times I

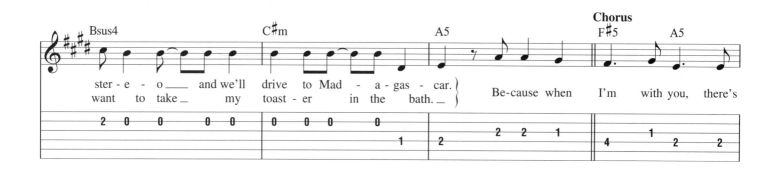

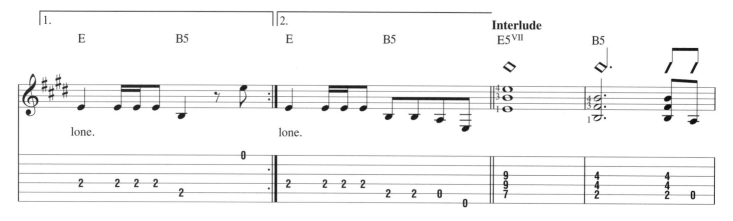

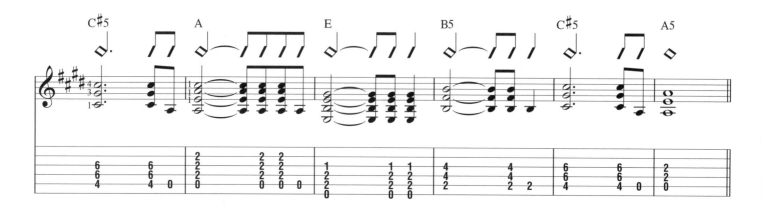

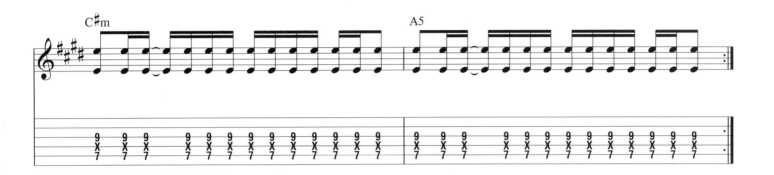

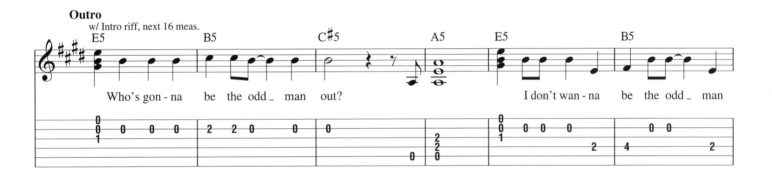

Outro
w/ Intro riff, next 16 meas.

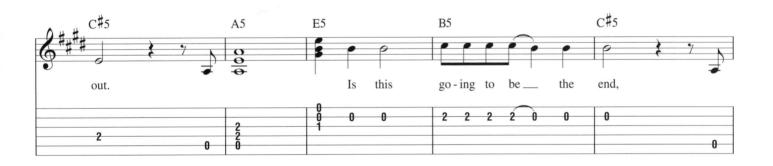

Who's gon - na be the odd _ man out? I don't wan - na be the odd _ man

out. Is this go - ing to be __ the end,

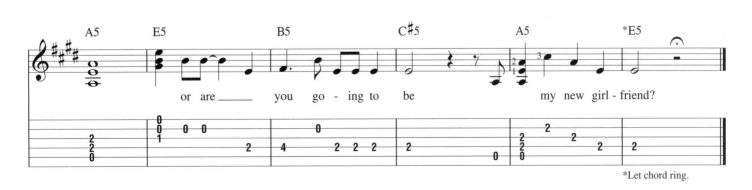

or are _____ you go - ing to be my new girl - friend?

*Let chord ring.

Dammit

Words and Music by Scott Raynor, Mark Hoppus and Tom De Longe

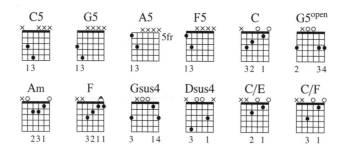

Strum Pattern: 2, 6
Pick Pattern: 4

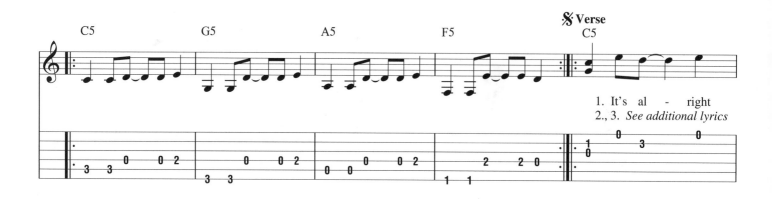

1. It's al - right
2., 3. *See additional lyrics*

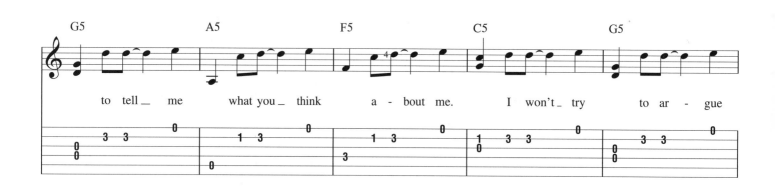

to tell __ me   what you __ think   a - bout me.   I won't __ try   to ar - gue

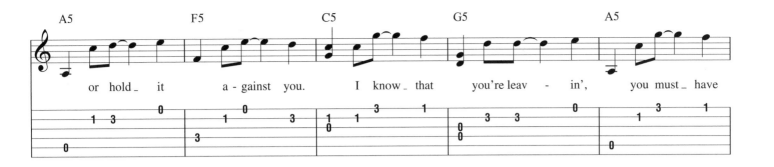

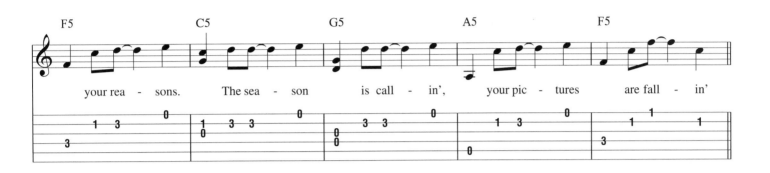

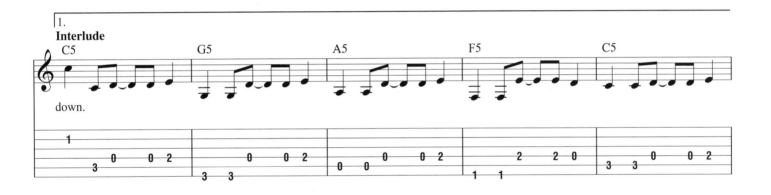

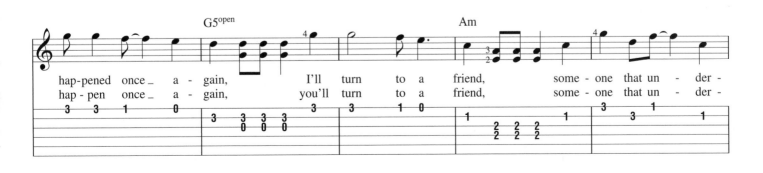

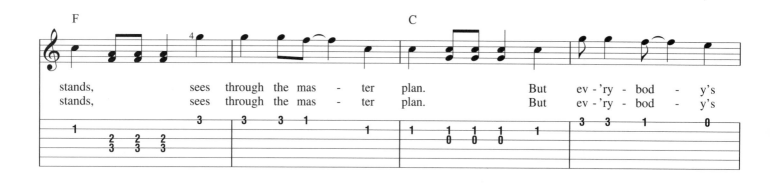

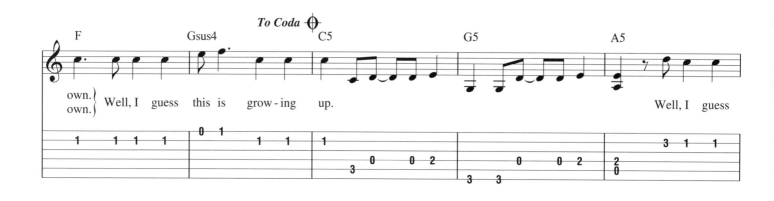

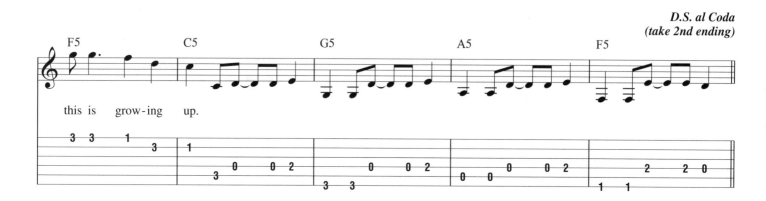

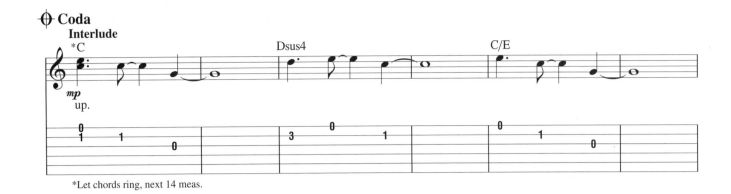

*Let chords ring, next 14 meas.

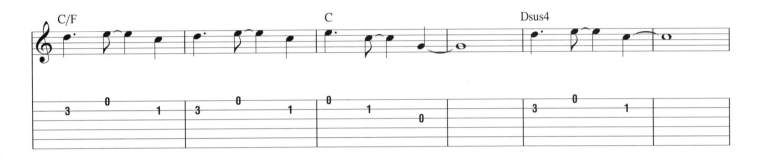

Well, I guess this is grow-ing up.

*Let chord ring.

Additional Lyrics

2. The steps that I retrace the sad look on your face.
   The timing and structure. Did you hear? He fucked her.
   A day late, a buck short. I'm writing the report
   On losing and fallin'. When I move I'm flailing now.

3. And maybe I'll see you at a movie sneak preview.
   You'll show up and walk by on the arm of that guy.
   And I'll smile and you'll wave, we'll pretend it's okay.
   The charade, it won't last. When he's gone, I won't come back.

What's My Age Again?

Words and Music by Tom DeLonge and Mark Hoppus

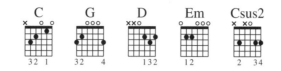

*Strum Pattern: 2
*Pick Pattern: 4

Intro
Driving

*Use Pattern 10 for $\frac{2}{4}$ meas.

Verse

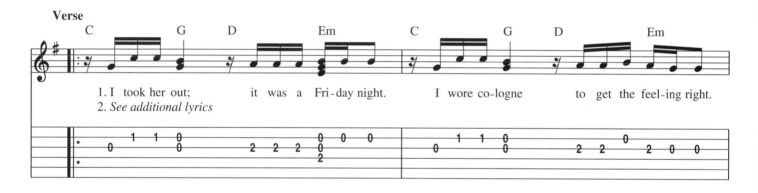

1. I took her out;   it was a Fri-day night.   I wore co-logne   to get the feel-ing right.
2. *See additional lyrics*

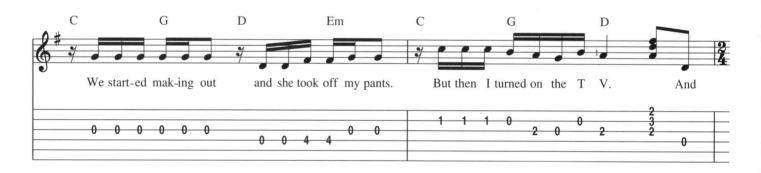

We start-ed mak-ing out   and she took off my pants.   But then I turned on the T. V.   And

Chorus

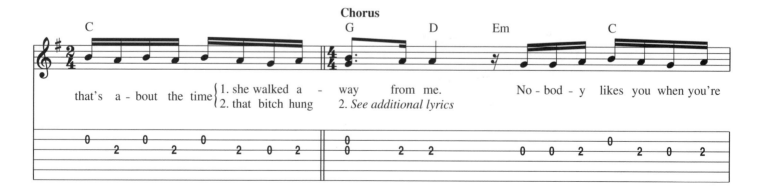

that's a-bout the time { 1. she walked a - way   from me.   No-bod-y likes you when you're
                         { 2. that bitch hung   2. *See additional lyrics*

twen - ty-three   and are still more a-mused by T V shows.   What the hell is A D D? My

friends say   I should act   my age.   What's my age   a - gain?   What's my age   a - gain?

1.

2.
Interlude

Em   D   C   D

Em   D   C   D

Em   D   C   D

Em   D   C   D

3. And that's a-bout the time she walked a -

Chorus

way   from me.   No-bod-y likes you when you're twen - ty-three   and you still act like you're in

4. *See additional lyrics*

fresh - man   year.   What the hell   is   wrong with me? My   friends say   I   should act   my   age.

What's my age a-gain?   What's my age   a-gain?

What's my age a-gain?   What's my age a-gain?

4. That's a-bout   the time that she broke

Play 3 times

What's my age a-gain?_____

Additional Lyrics

2. Then later on, on the drive home,
I called her mom from a pay phone.
I said I was the cops and your husband's in jail.
This state looks down on sodomy.

Chorus 2. And that's about the time that bitch hung up on me.
Nobody likes you when you're twenty-three
And are still more amused by prank phone calls.
What the hell is call ID?
My friends say I should act my age.
What's my age again? What's my age again?

Chorus 4. That's about the time that she broke up with me.
No one should take themselves so seriously.
With many years ahead to fall in line,
Why would you wish that on me?
I never wanna act my age.
What's my age again? What's my age again?

Feeling This

Words and Music by Travis Barker, Tom De Longe and Mark Hoppus

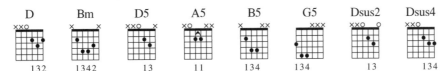

Strum Pattern: 1, 4
Pick Pattern: 4

Intro
Very fast

Spoken: 1. I

§ Verse

got no regret right now.
Spoken: 2. Where do we go right from here?

I'm feelin' this. The air is so cold and low.
Turn all the lights down now.

I'm feelin' this. Let me go in her room.
Smiling from ear to ear.

I'm feelin' this. I
I'm feelin' this. Our

wanna take off her clothes.
breathing has got too loud.

I'm feelin' this. Show me the way to bed.
I'm feelin' this. Show me the bedroom floor.

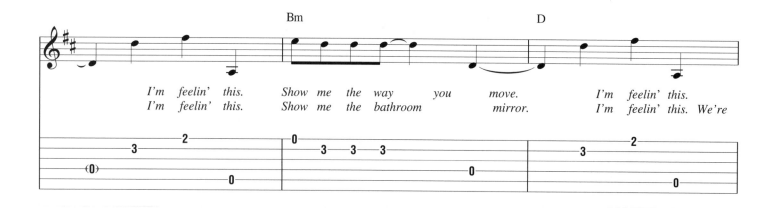

I'm feelin' this. Show me the way you move. I'm feelin' this.
I'm feelin' this. Show me the bathroom mirror. I'm feelin' this. We're

Fuck it, it's such a blur. I'm feelin' this. I love all the things you do. I'm feelin' this.
taking this way too slow. I'm feelin' this. Take me away from here. I'm feelin' this.

Chorus

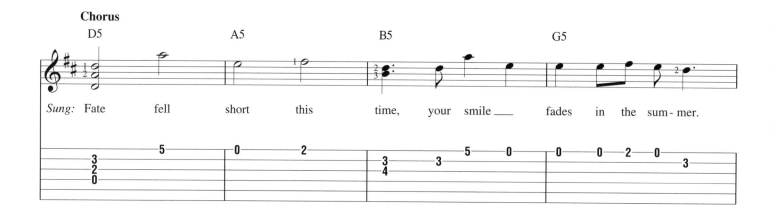

Sung: Fate fell short this time, your smile ___ fades in the sum-mer.

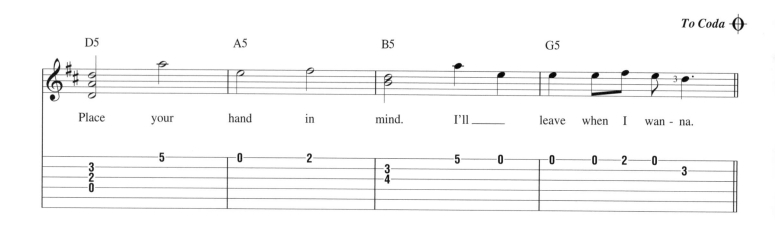

Place your hand in mind. I'll ___ leave when I wan-na.

Interlude

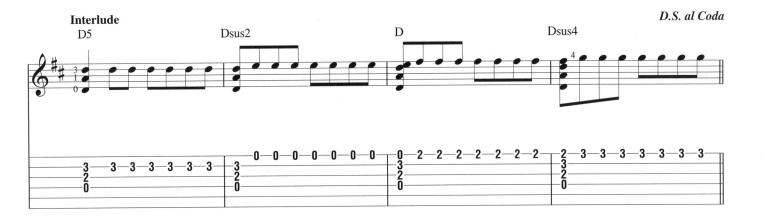

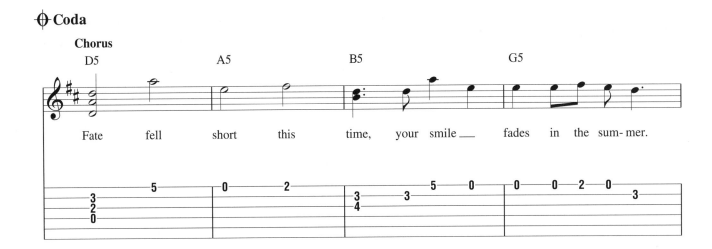

Bridge

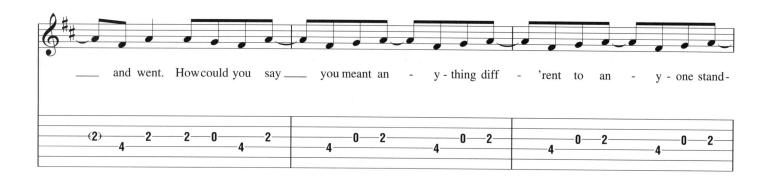

_____ and went. How could you say _____ you meant an - y - thing diff - - 'rent to an - y - one stand-

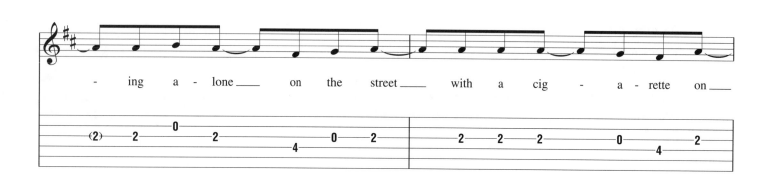

- ing a - lone _____ on the street _____ with a cig - a - rette on _____

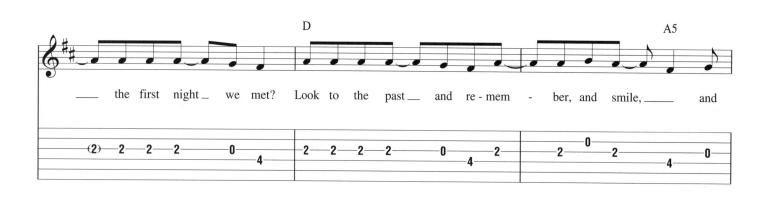

_____ the first night _ we met? Look to the past _ and re - mem - ber, and smile, _____ and

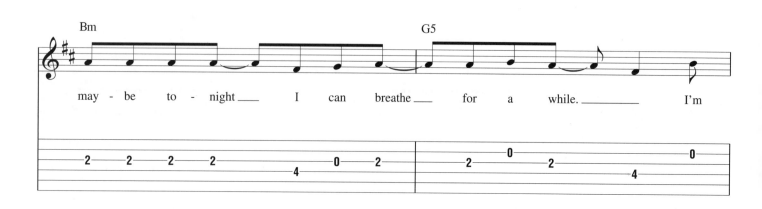

may - be to - night _____ I can breathe _____ for a while. _____ I'm

not in the scene, ___ I think I'm fall - ing a - sleep. ___ But then all ___

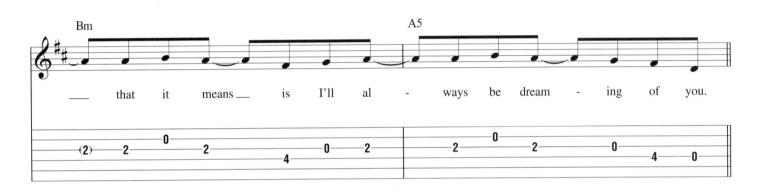

___ that it means ___ is I'll al - ways be dream - ing of you.

Outro-Chorus

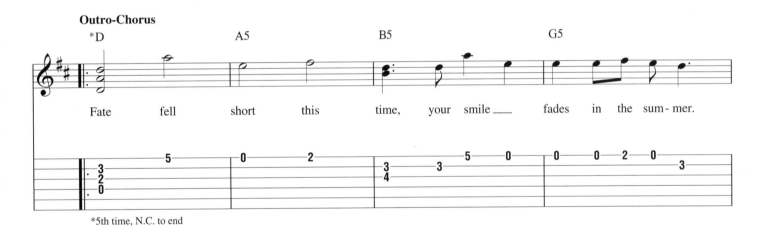

Fate fell short this time, your smile ___ fades in the sum - mer.

*5th time, N.C. to end

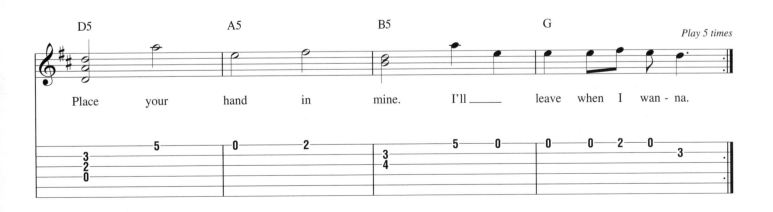

Place your hand in mine. I'll ___ leave when I wan - na.

All the Small Things

Words and Music by Tom De Longe and Mark Hoppus

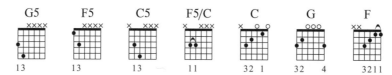

Strum Pattern: 1

Intro

Bright Rock

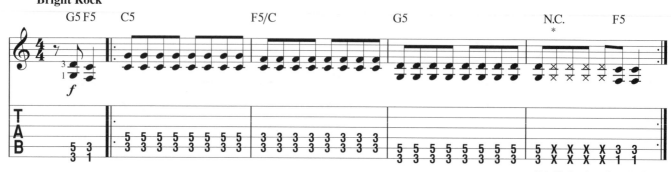

*Muffled strings: Lay the fret hand across the strings without depressing and strike them w/ the pick hand.

Verse

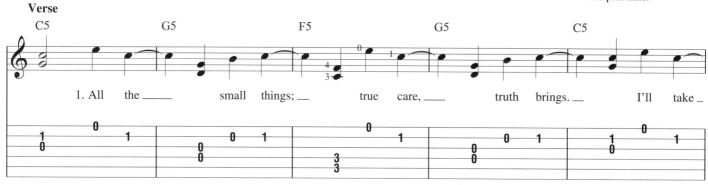

1. All the small things; true care, truth brings. I'll take

Verse

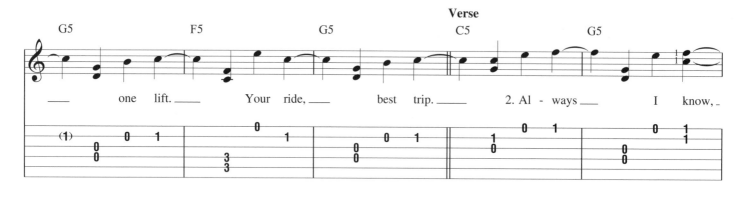

one lift. Your ride, best trip. 2. Al - ways I know,

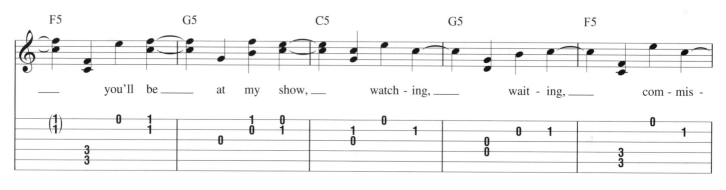

you'll be at my show, watch - ing, wait - ing, com - mis -

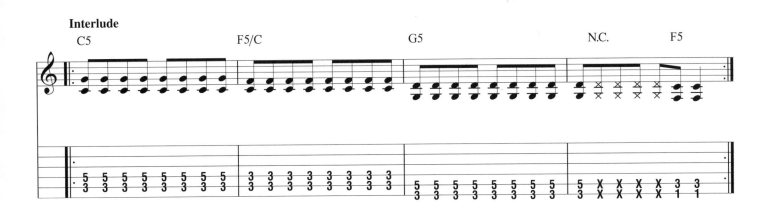

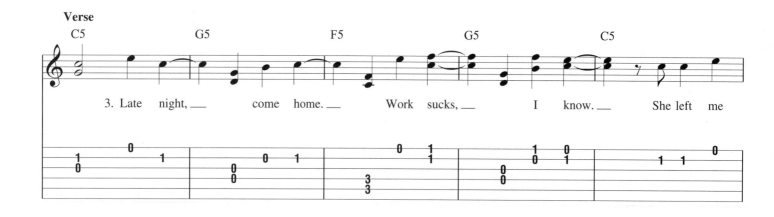

Verse

3. Late night, come home. Work sucks, I know. She left me

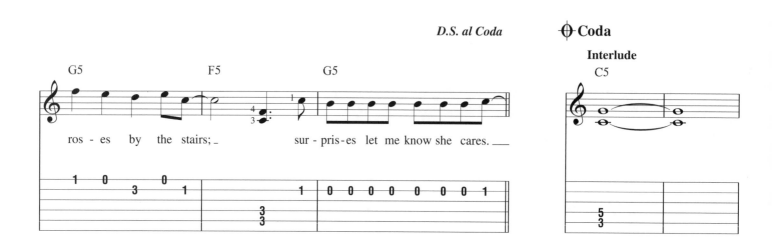

D.S. al Coda ⊕ **Coda**

Interlude

ros - es by the stairs; sur - pris - es let me know she cares.

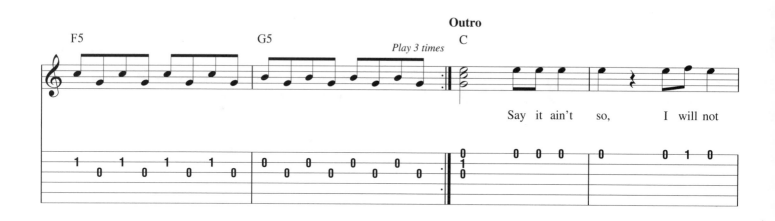

Outro

Play 3 times

Say it ain't so, I will not

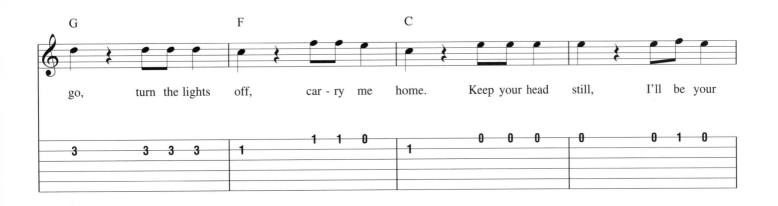

Adam's Song

Words and Music by Tom De Longe and Mark Hoppus

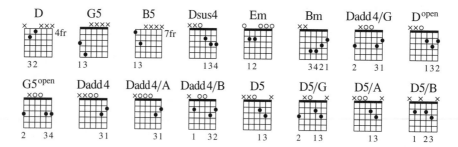

*Tune down 1 step:
(low to high) D-G-C-F-A-D

Strum Pattern: 1, 6
Pick Pattern: 2

Intro
Moderate Rock

*Optional: To match recording, tune down 1 step.

Verse

1. I nev - er thought __ I'd die a - lone. __ I laughed the loud - est. Who'd have known? __
2. *See additional lyrics*

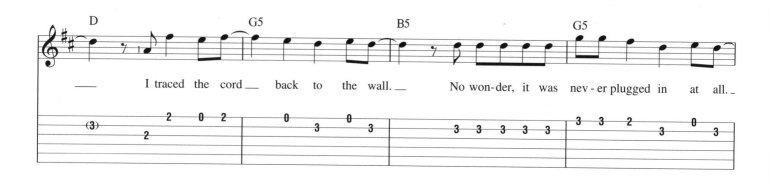

__ I traced the cord __ back to the wall. __ No won - der, it was nev - er plugged in at all. __

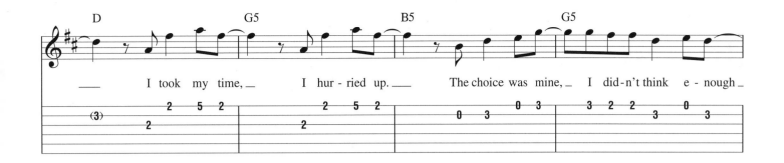

I took my time, __ I hur - ried up. __ The choice was mine, __ I did-n't think e - nough __

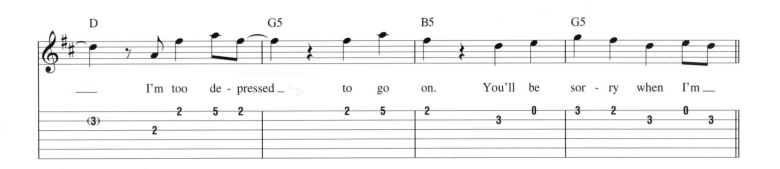

I'm too de - pressed __ to go on. You'll be sor - ry when I'm __

Interlude

gone. _____

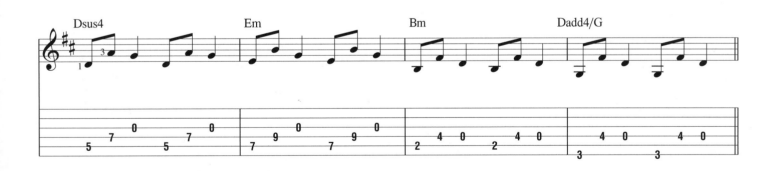

𝄆 Chorus

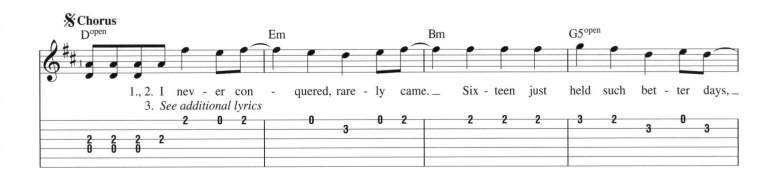

1., 2. I nev - er con - quered, rare - ly came. __ Six - teen just held such bet - ter days, __
3. *See additional lyrics*

days when I _____ still felt a-live. ____ We could-n't wait to get ____ out-

side. The world __ was wide, __ too late __ to try. ___ The tour was o - ver, we'd sur - vived. __

To Coda ⊕ |1.

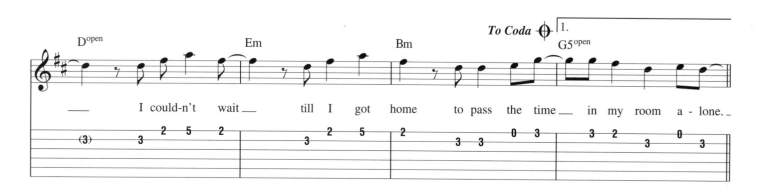

I could-n't wait __ till I got home to pass the time __ in my room a - lone. __

Interlude

N.C.(Bm)

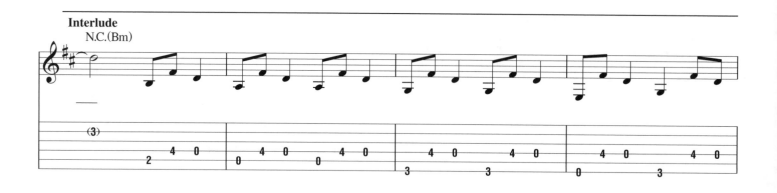

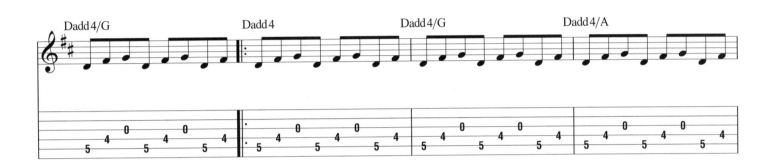

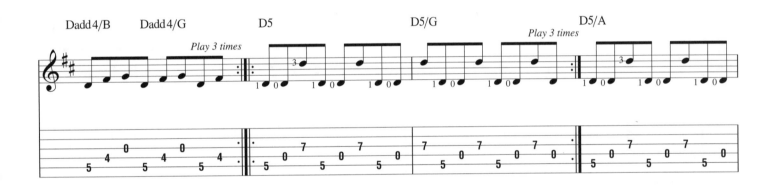

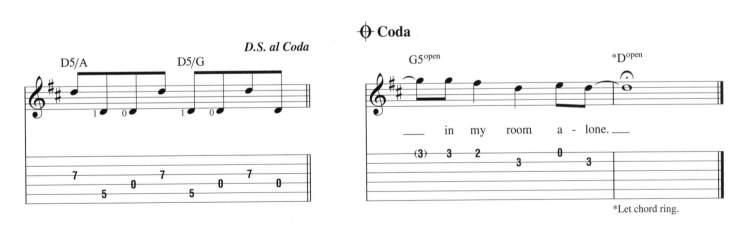

*Let chord ring.

Additional Lyrics

2. I never thought I'd die alone.
Another six months I'll be unknown.
Give all my things to all my friends.
You'll never step foot in my room again.
You'll close it off, board it up.
Remember the time that I spilled the cup
Of apple juice in the hall?
Please tell Mom this is not her fault.

Chorus 3. I never conquered, rarely came.
But tomorrow holds such better days,
Days when I can still feel alive,
When I can't wait to get outside.
The world is wide, the time goes by.
The tour is over, I've survived.
I can't wait till I get home
To pass the time in my room alone.

Man Overboard

Words and Music by Tom De Longe and Mark Hoppus

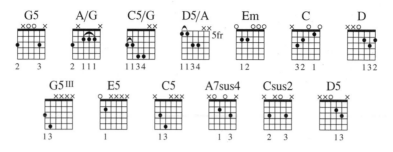

Strum Pattern: 1, 2
Pick Pattern: 5

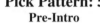

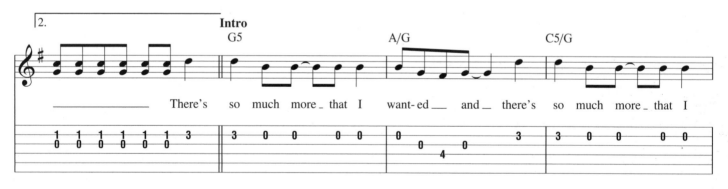

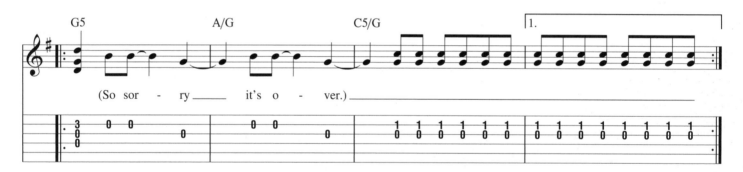

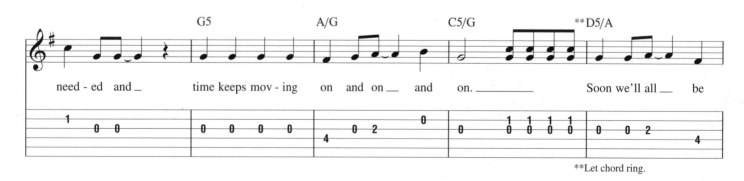

**Let chord ring.

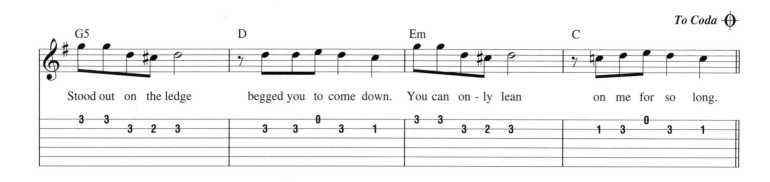

Stood out on the ledge   begged you to come down.   You can on-ly lean   on me for so   long.

2nd time, D.S. al Coda

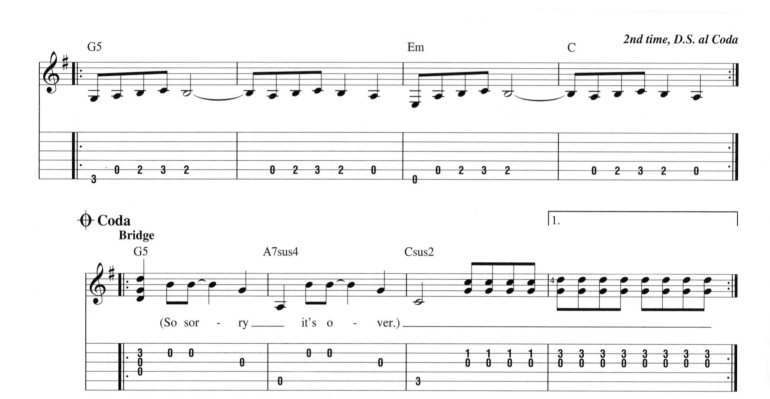

⊕ **Coda**

Bridge

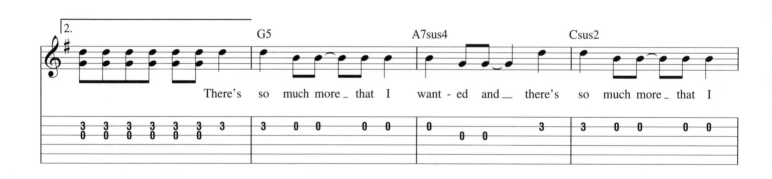

(So sor - ry ___ it's o - ver.) ___

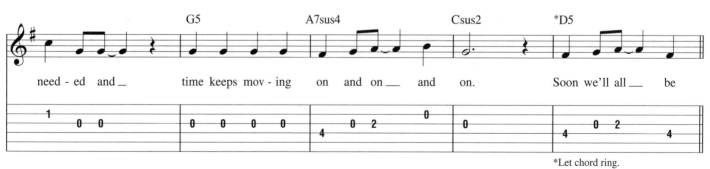

There's   so   much more _ that   I   want - ed   and _ there's   so   much more _ that   I

need - ed   and _   time keeps mov - ing   on   and on __   and   on.   Soon we'll all __ be

*Let chord ring.

*Let chord ring.

Additional Lyrics

2. I remember shots without a chaser.
Absent-minded thoughts, now you're a stranger?
Cover up the scars, put on your game face.
Left you in the bar to try and save face.

The Rock Show

Words and Music by Tom De Longe, Mark Hoppus and Travis Barker

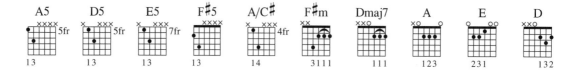

Strum Pattern: 4
Pick Pattern: 1

Intro
Fast Rock

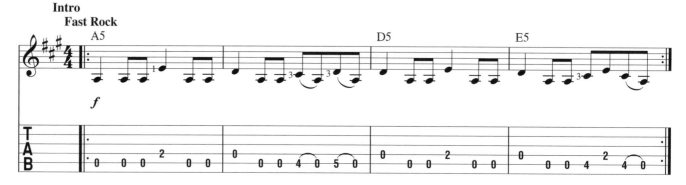

1. Hang-ing out be-hind the

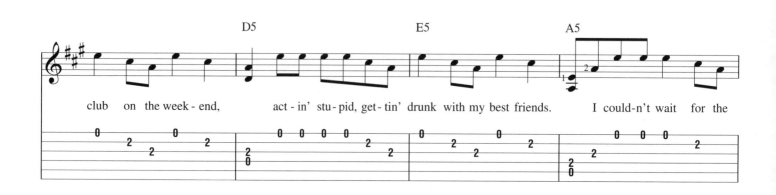

club on the week-end, act-in' stu-pid, get-tin' drunk with my best friends. I could-n't wait for the

sum - mer and the Warped Tour. I re - mem - ber it's the first time that I saw her there.

Interlude

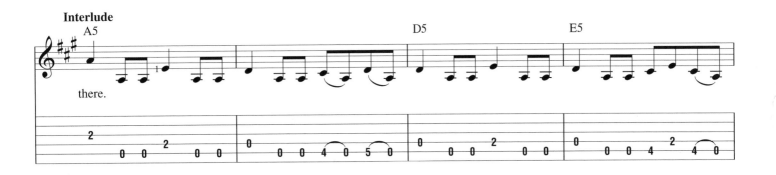

there.

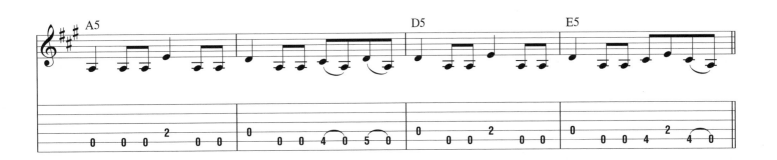

𝄋 Verse

2. She's get - tin' kicked out of school 'cause she's fail - ing. I'm kind - a ner - vous 'cause I
3. *See additional lyrics*

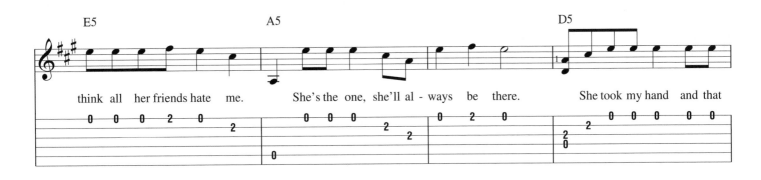

think all her friends hate me. She's the one, she'll al - ways be there. She took my hand and that

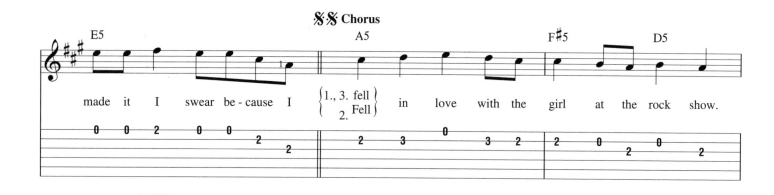

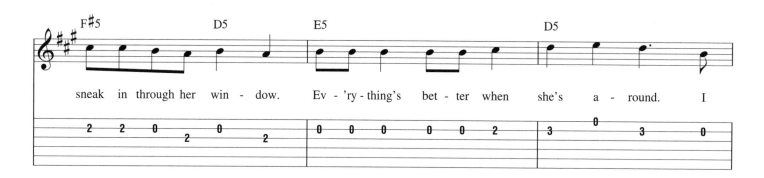

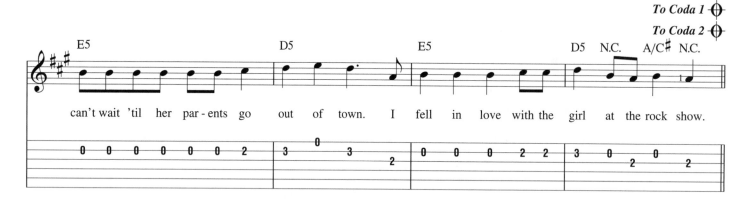

To Coda 1 ⊕

To Coda 2 ⊕

2nd time, D.S. al Coda 1

Interlude

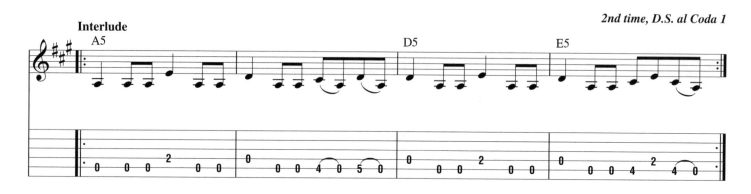

Coda 1

Bridge

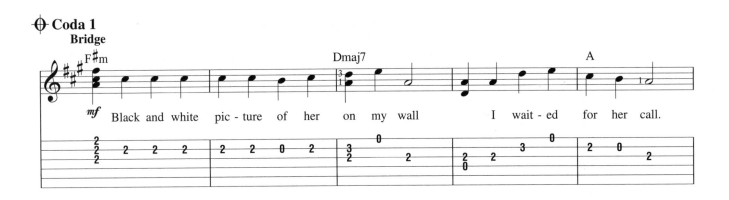

Black and white pic-ture of her on my wall   I wait-ed for her call.

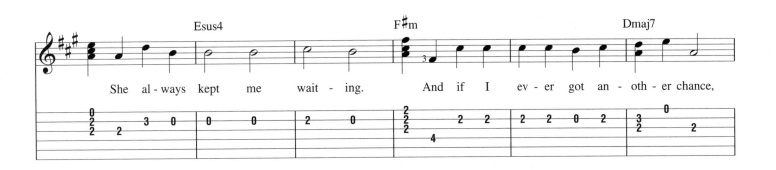

She al-ways kept me wait - ing.   And if I ev - er got an - oth - er chance,

D.S.S. al Coda 2

I'd still ask her to dance   be - cause she kept me wait - ing. I

Coda 2

Repeat and fade

Outro
w/ Intro riff

With the girl at the rock show.

Additional Lyrics

3. When we said we were gonna move to Vegas,
   I remember the look her mother gave us.
   Seventeen without a purpose or direction.
   We don't owe anyone a fuckin' explanation.

First Date

Words and Music by Tom De Longe, Mark Hoppus and Travis Barker

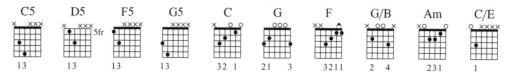

Strum Pattern: 1, 5
Pick Pattern: 4

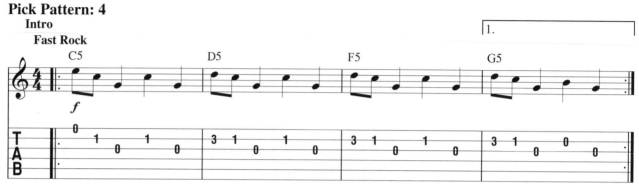

1. In the car   I   just can't   wait _   to pick you up   on our
2. *See additional lyrics*

ver-y first date.   Is it cool if I hold your hand?   Is it wrong if I

think it's lame to dance?   Do you like   my stu-pid hair? _   Would you guess that I

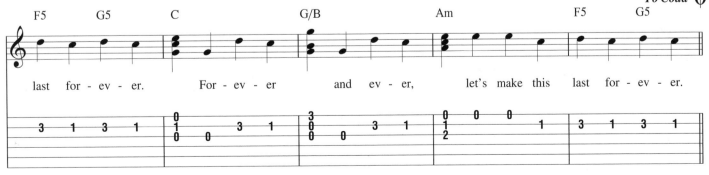

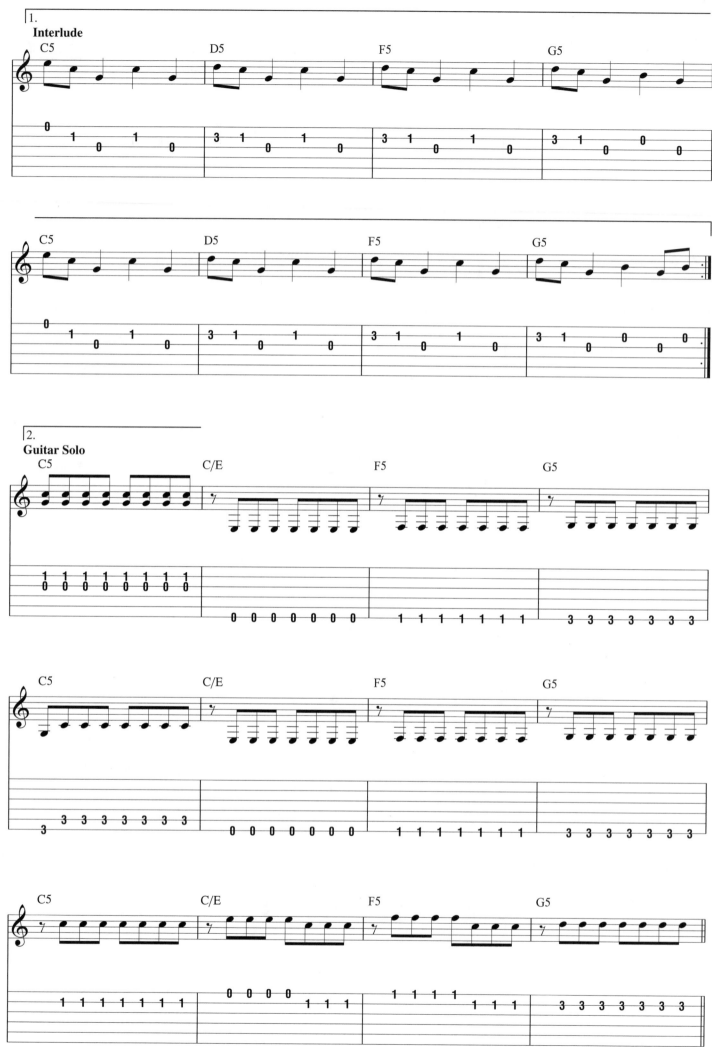

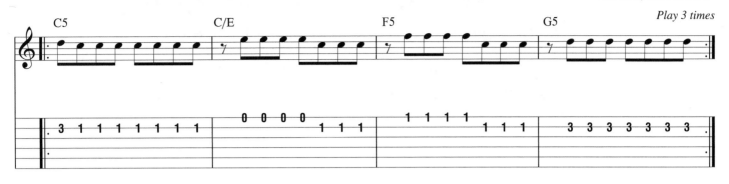

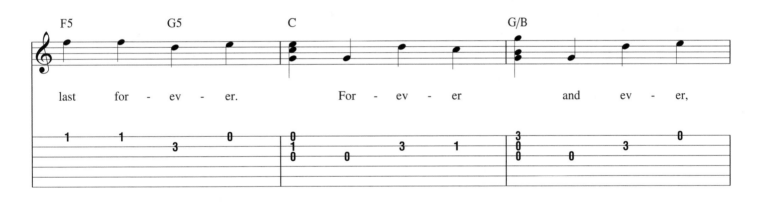

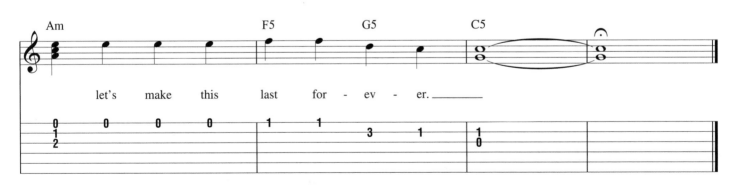

Additional Lyrics

2. When you smile, I melt inside.
   I'm not worthy for a minute of your time.
   I really wish it was only me and you.
   I'm jealous of ev'rybody in the room.
   Please don't look at me with those eyes.
   Please don't hint that you're capable of lies.
   I dread the thought of our very first kiss,
   A target that I'm prob'ly gonna miss.

Stay Together for the Kids

Words and Music by Tom De Longe, Mark Hoppus and Travis Barker

Strum Pattern: 1
Pick Pattern: 5

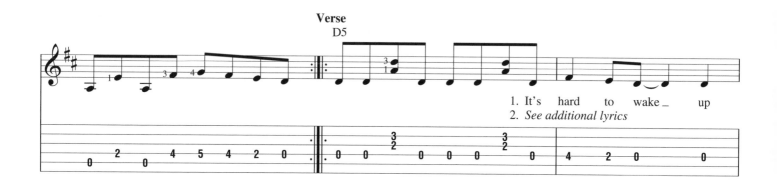

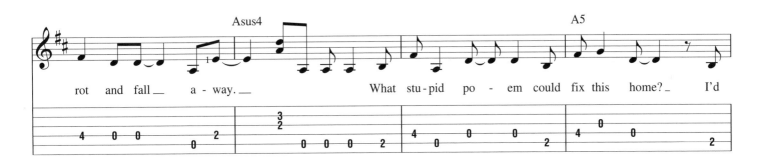

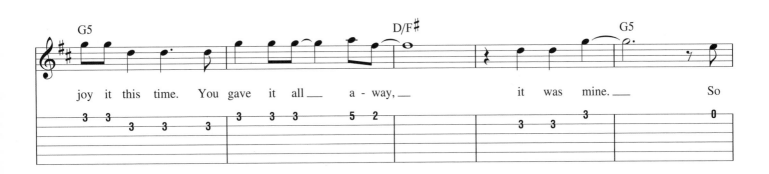

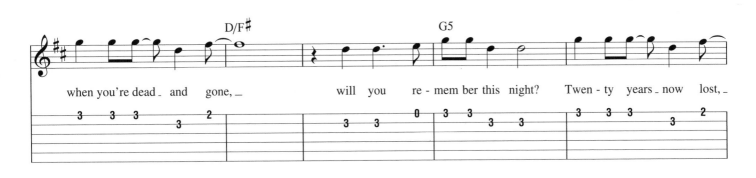

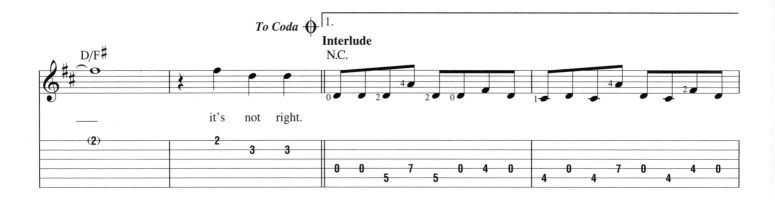

it's   not   right.

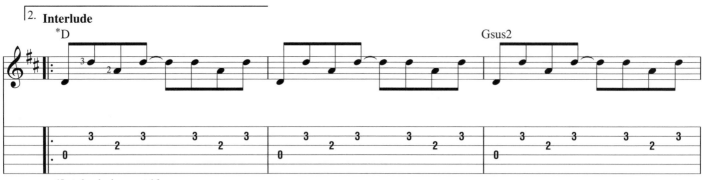

*Let chords ring, next 16 meas.

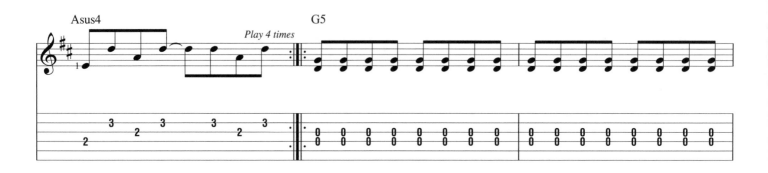

So

Coda
Outro

It's not right. It's not right.

It's not right.

Repeat and fade

Additional Lyrics

2. Their anger hurts my ears,
   Been runnin' strong for seven years.
   Rather than fix the problems
   They never solve them.
   It makes no sense at all.
   I see them ev'ry day.
   We get along, so why can't they?
   If this is what he wants
   And it's what she wants,
   Then why is there so much pain?

I Miss You

Words and Music by Travis Barker, Tom De Longe and Mark Hoppus

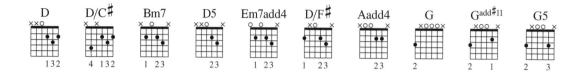

*Tune down 1 1/2 steps:
(low to high) C#-F#-B-E-G#-C#

Strum Pattern: 3, 6
Pick Pattern: 2, 5

Intro
Moderately

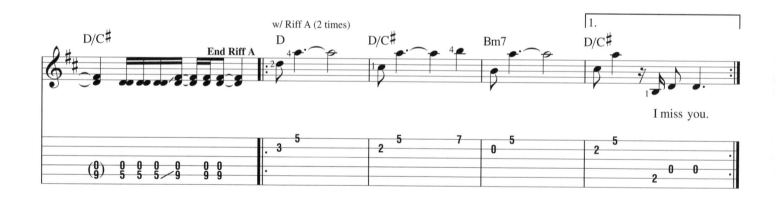

*Optional: To match recording, tune down 1 1/2 steps.

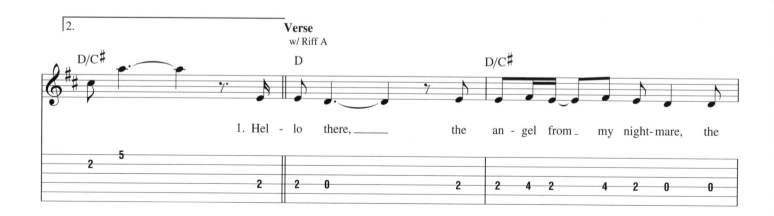

I miss you.

1. Hel - lo there, _____ the an - gel from _ my night-mare, the

shad - ow in the back - ground of the morgue, the un - sus-pect - ing vic - tim of

dark - ness in the val - ley, we can live like Jack and Sal - ly if we want

where you can al - ways find me. And we'll have Hal-low-een on Christ-mas, and

in the night we'll wish this nev - er ends, we'll wish this nev - er ends.

Chorus

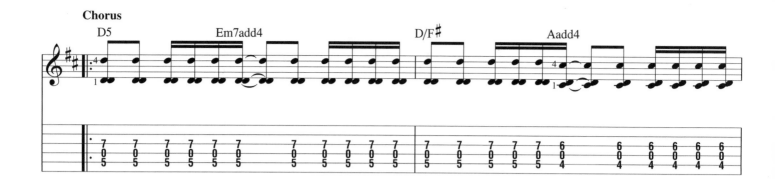

I miss you.   2. Where are ___

Verse

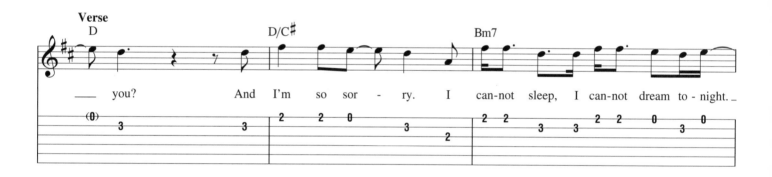

___ you?   And I'm so sor - ry.   I can-not sleep, I can-not dream to - night. ___

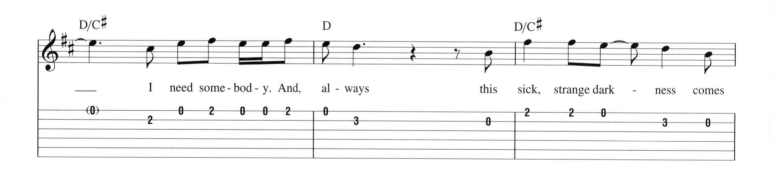

___ I need some-bod - y. And, al - ways   this sick, strange dark - ness comes

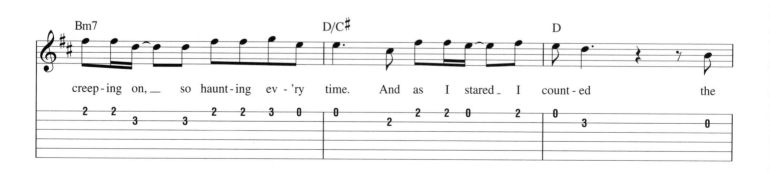

creep-ing on, ___ so haunt-ing ev - 'ry time. And as I stared ___ I count - ed   the

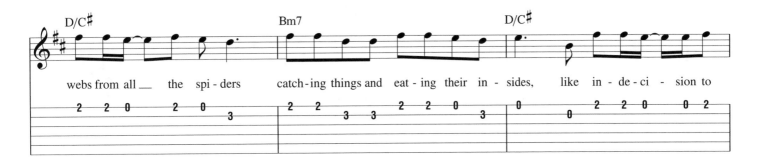

webs from all __ the spi - ders   catch-ing things and eat - ing their in - sides,   like in - de - ci - sion to

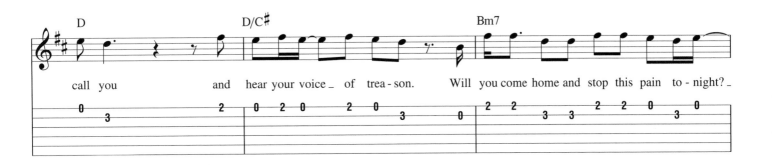

call you   and hear your voice _ of trea - son.   Will you come home and stop this pain to - night? _

__   Stop this pain to-night. Don't waste   your time   on   me, ___ you're al - read - y   the

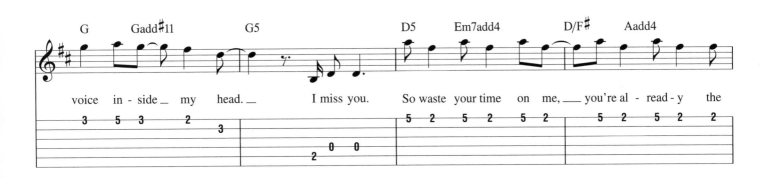

voice in - side __ my   head. __   I miss you.   So waste   your time   on   me, ___ you're al - read - y   the

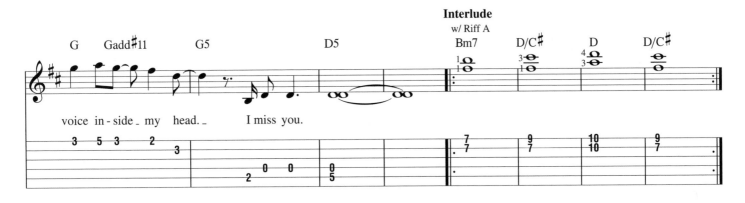

voice in - side _ my   head. __   I miss you.

Chorus

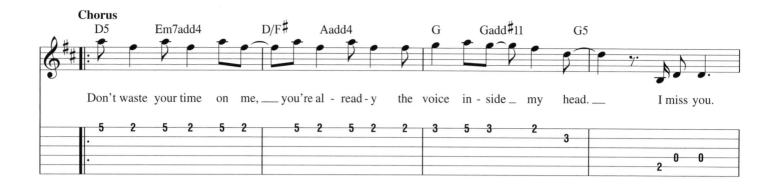

Don't waste your time on me, __ you're al - read - y the voice in - side __ my head. __ I miss you.

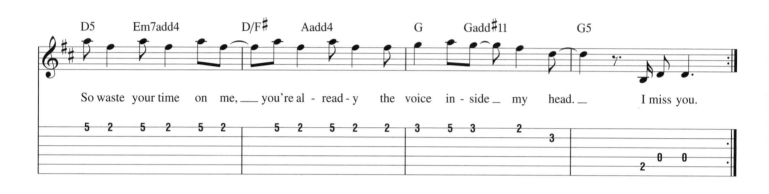

So waste your time on me, __ you're al - read - y the voice in - side __ my head. __ I miss you.

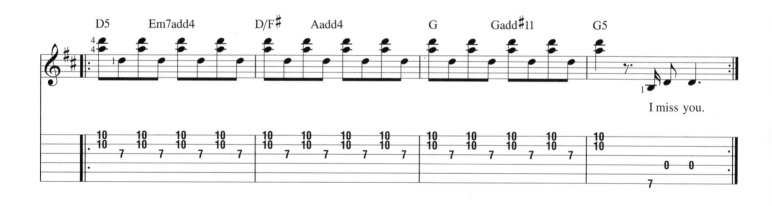

I miss you.

Repeat and fade

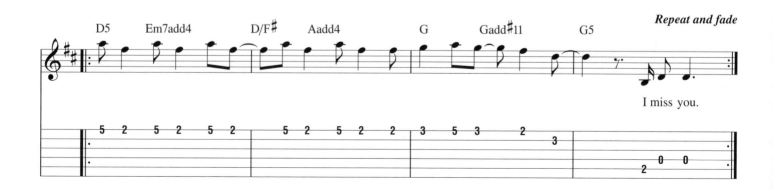

I miss you.

Down

Words and Music by Travis Barker, Tom De Longe and Mark Hoppus

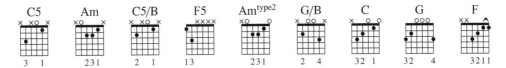

*Tune down 1/2 step:
(low to high) E♭-A♭-D♭-G♭-B♭-E♭

Strum Pattern: 2, 4
Pick Pattern: 6

Intro
Moderately fast

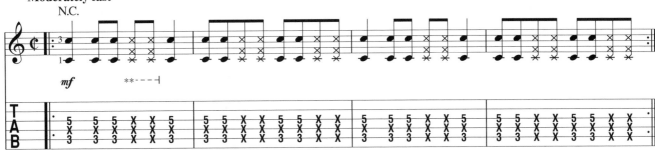

*Optional: To match recording, tune down 1/2 step.
**Strum muted strings where indicated.

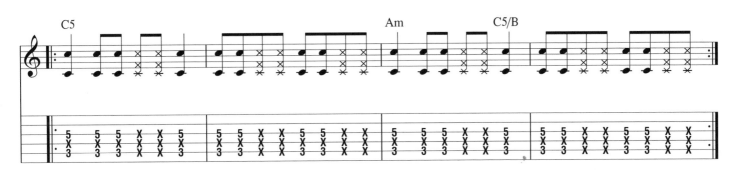

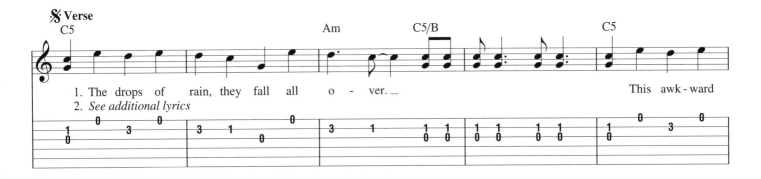

1. The drops of rain, they fall all o - ver. ___ This awk - ward

2. *See additional lyrics*

si - lence makes me cra - zy. ___ The glow in - side burns light up -

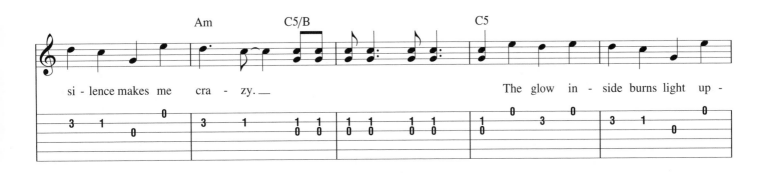

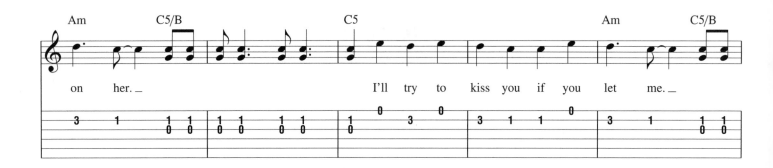

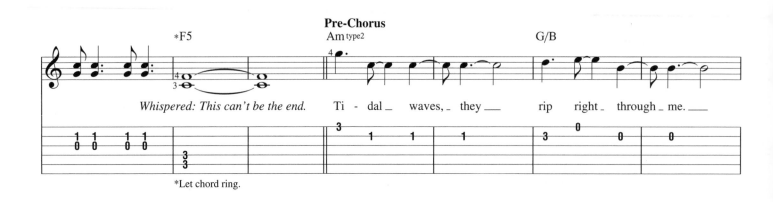

*Let chord ring.

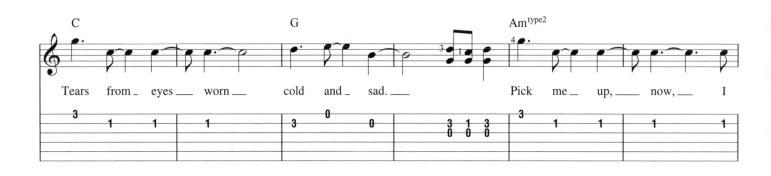

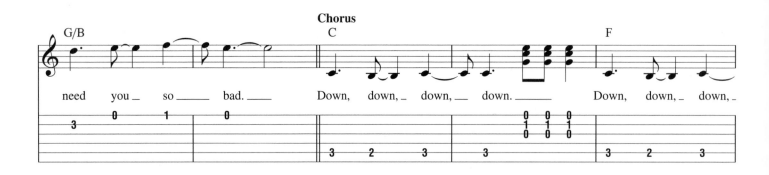

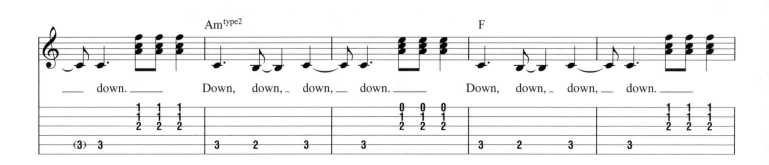

Additional Lyrics

2. Your vows of silence fall all over.
   The look in your eyes makes me crazy.
   I feel the darkness break upon her.
   I'll take you over if you let me.
   Whispered: You did this.

Always

Words and Music by Travis Barker, Tom De Longe and Mark Hoppus

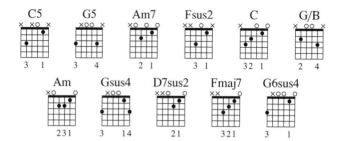

*Tune down 1/2 step:
(low to high) Eb-Ab-Db-Gb-Bb-Eb

Strum Pattern: 1, 6
Pick Pattern: 2

Intro
Fast

*Optional: To match recording, tune down 1/2 step.

1. I've been here ___ be - fore ___ a few ___ times, ___
2. *See additional lyrics*

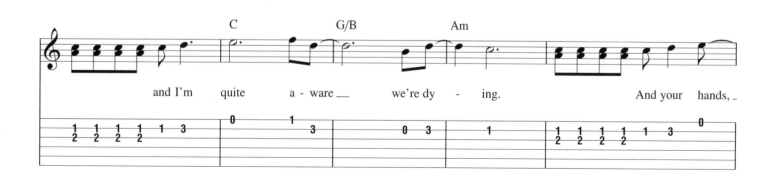

and I'm quite a - ware ___ we're dy - ing. And your hands, ___

they shake with good - byes. And I'll take __ you back if you'd have __

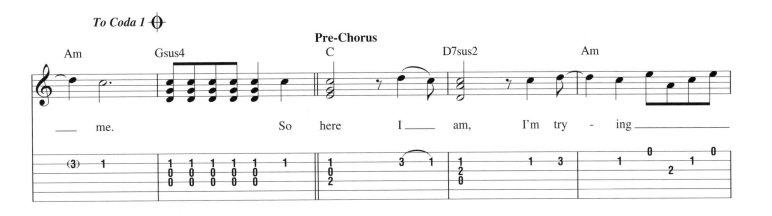

__ me. So here I __ am, I'm try - ing __

So here I __ am are you read - y? __

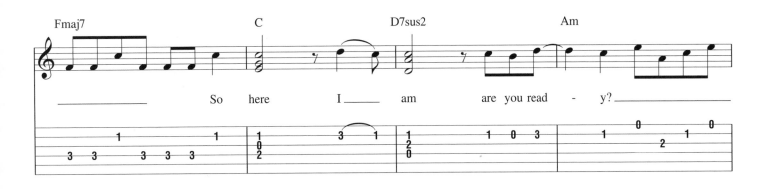

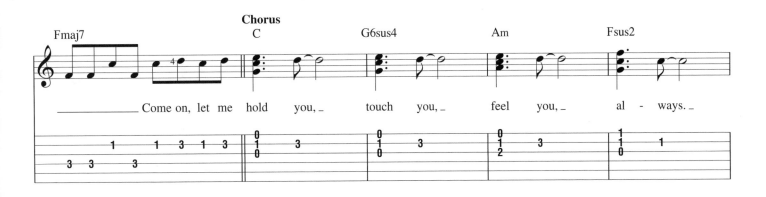

__ Come on, let me hold you, __ touch you, __ feel you, __ al - ways.

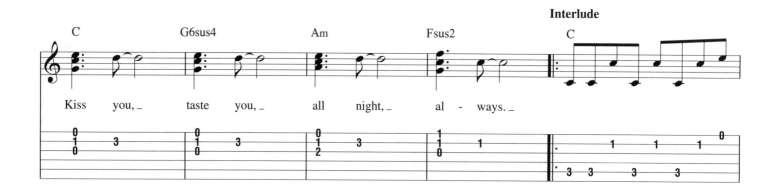

Kiss you, — taste you, — all night, — al - ways. —

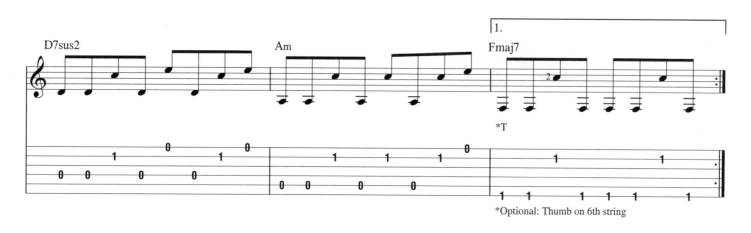

*Optional: Thumb on 6th string

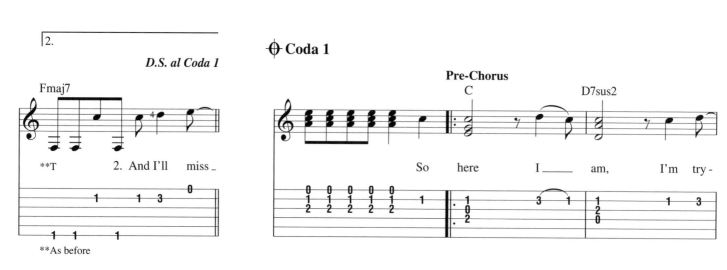

D.S. al Coda 1

2. And I'll miss —

**As before

✛ **Coda 1**

So here I — am, I'm try-

- ing. _____ So here I — am, are you read -

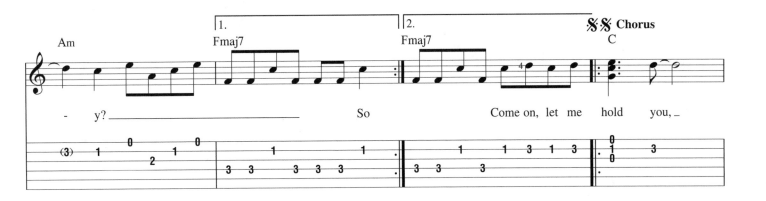

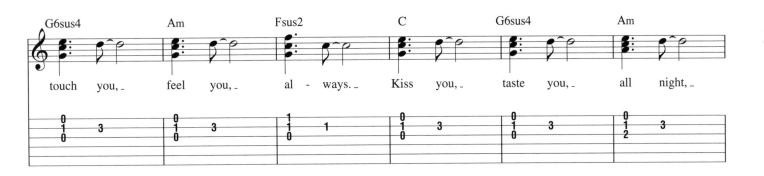

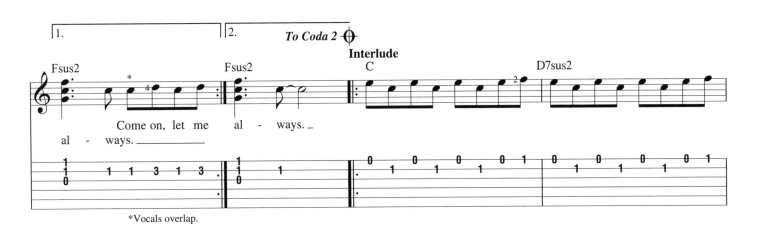

*Vocals overlap.

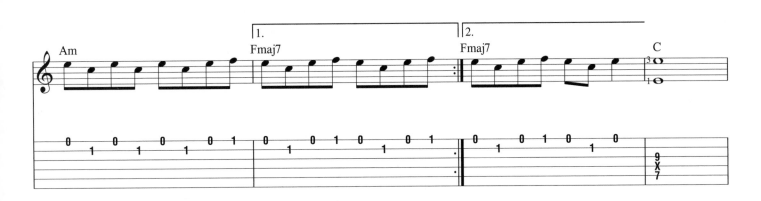

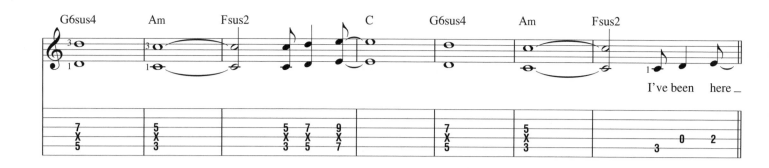

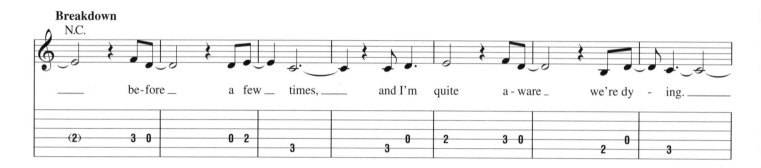

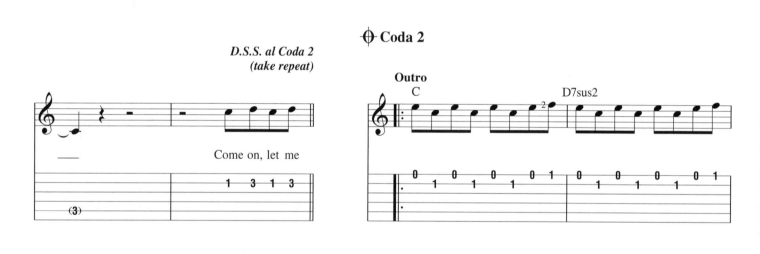

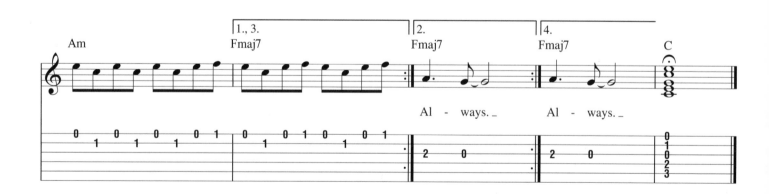

Additional Lyrics

2. And I'll miss your laugh, your smile.
   I'll admit I'm wrong if you'd tell me.
   I'm so sick of fights, I hate them.
   Let's start this again for real.

Not Now

Words and Music by Mark Hoppus, Tom De Longe and Travis Barker

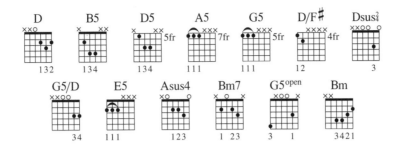

Drop D tuning:
(low to high) D-A-D-G-B-E

Strum Pattern: 1, 6
Pick Pattern: 4

Intro
Fast Rock

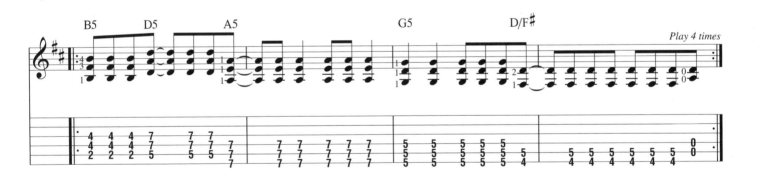

Verse

1. Come here, _____ please hold my hand _ for now. Help me. _____ I'm scared, please

*Let chords ring, next 16 meas.

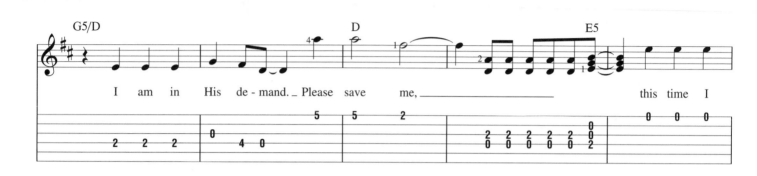

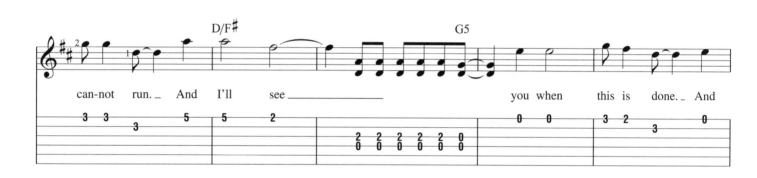

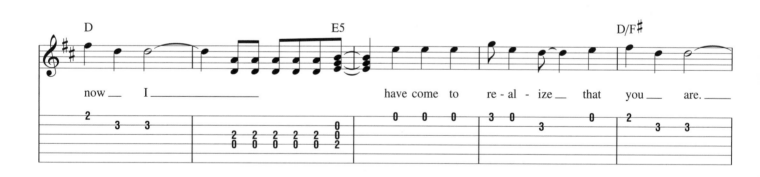

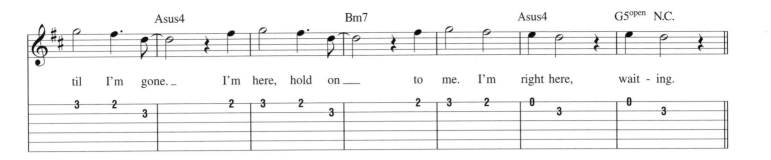

*Let chords ring, next 16 meas.

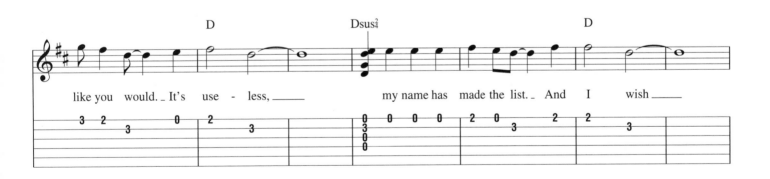

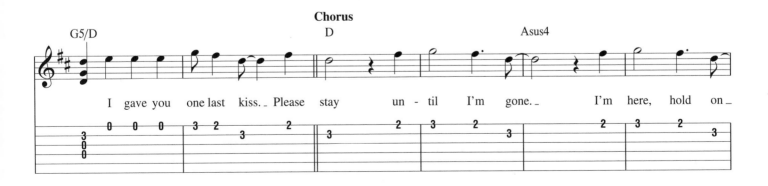

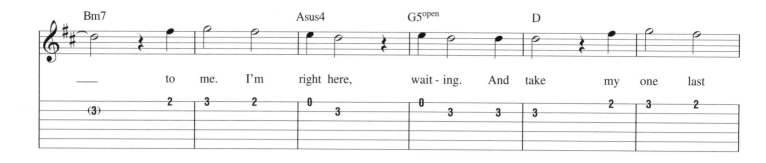

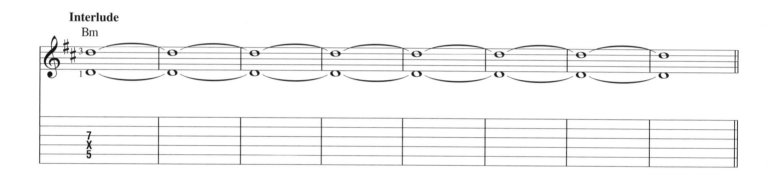

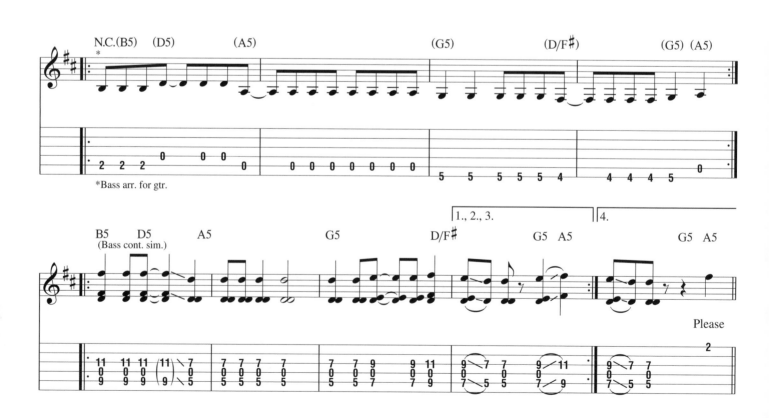

Chorus

stay un-til I'm gone. ___ I'm here, hold on ___ to me. I'm right here,

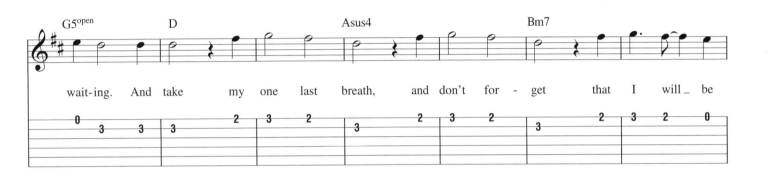

wait-ing. And take my one last breath, and don't for-get that I will ___ be

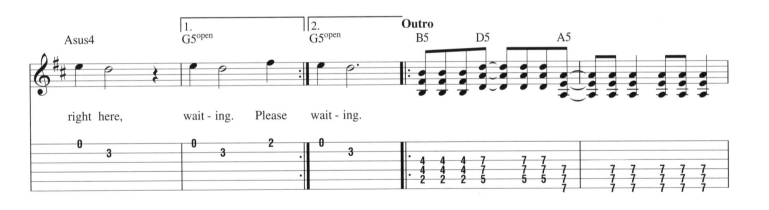

right here, wait-ing. Please wait-ing.

Another Girl Another Planet

Words and Music by Peter Perrett

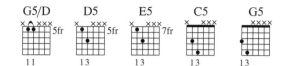

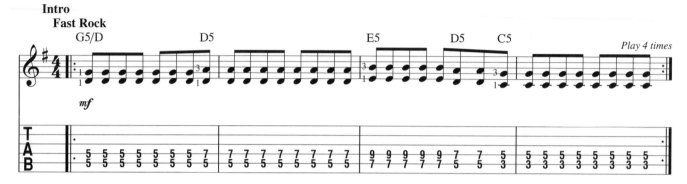

Strum Pattern: 1, 6
Pick Pattern: 2

Intro
Fast Rock

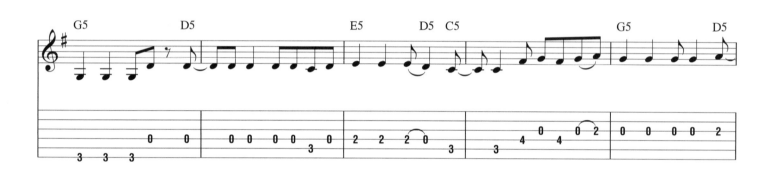

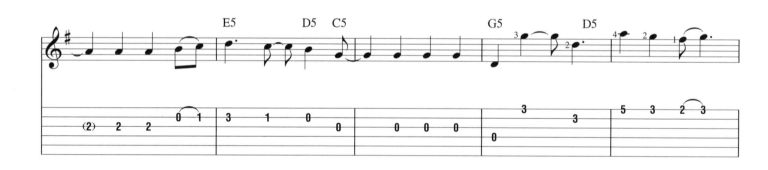

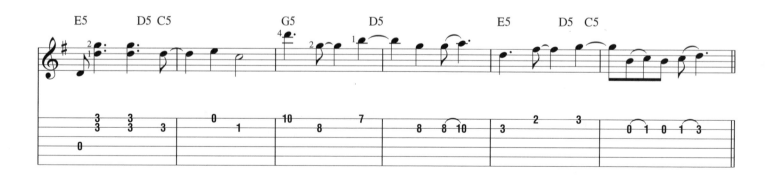

Additional Lyrics

2. You always get under my skin, I don't find it irritating. 3. Space travel's in my blood, and there ain't nothing I can do about it.
You always play to win, I don't need rehabilitating. Long journeys wear me out. Oh, God, you know we won't live without it.